TEACH YOURSELF BOOKS

MUSIC

Thousands of people feel the urge to play, to sing, to compose, to make or create music, but are put off by the supposed drudgery of learning, or simply because they do not know how to make a start. The whole purpose of this book is to smooth out some of the practical difficulties that lie in the path of the would-be performer. No technical knowledge of music on the reader's part is presumed.

It is a first-rate and unique contribution to the teaching of music.

The Schoolmaster

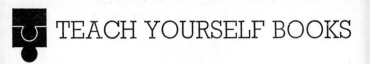
TEACH YOURSELF BOOKS

MUSIC

King Palmer

Associate of the Royal Academy of Music

ST. PAUL'S HOUSE WARWICK LANE LONDON EC4P 4AH

First printed	1944
Third edition	1965
Fourth edition	1971
Second impression	1973

Copyright © 1965, 1971 editions
The English Universities Press Ltd.

All rights reserved. No part of this publication may be reproduced or transmitted in any form or by any means, electronic or mechanical, including photocopy, recording, or any information storage and retrieval system, without permission in writing from the publisher.

ISBN 0 340 05666 5

Printed in Great Britain for
The English Universities Press Ltd., London, by
Elliott Bros. & Yeoman Ltd., Liverpool, L24 9JL.

PREFACE

Penelope Prim tripped out of the house, proudly clutching a brown leather music case. She was light of step and heart, for to-day was her eighth birthday, and she was on her way to her first music lesson. Her father viewed the project with some misgivings, and it was only Penelope's passionate pleadings that at last persuaded him to give it his blessing. When Penelope returned from her lesson, and commenced to practise five finger exercises with energy and determination, his doubts were allayed but not removed. The exercises continued with great regularity for several days, after which they became more and more spasmodic, and ended with the transfer of Penelope's interests to butterfly collecting. When Penelope grew up, she often felt that she would like to take up the piano again, but somehow she could never bear the thought of those five finger exercises.

Penelope, of course, is an entirely imaginary young lady, but there are thousands of people who, like her, feel the urge to play or to sing, but are put off by the supposed drudgery of learning, or simply because they do not know how to make a start. The whole purpose of this book is to smooth out some of the practical difficulties that lie in the path of the would-be performer. Many admirable books have been written on the art of listening to and enjoying music. This study of musical appreciation has largely been fostered by the remarkable revival of interest in music, during the past ten years or so. But may not this emphasis on the passive art of listening have the effect of diverting many from the active pursuits of playing and singing ? For listening has become too easy ; a turn of a knob, and the most accomplished performers, the most brilliant compositions, are at our call.

But where the making of music is concerned, things are by no means so easy. The potential performer is able to buy an album of piano studies, a tutor for the oboe, a book on singing or the organ, but how on earth is he to know which instrument or subject he ought to study, when he may have only the vaguest idea of what an organ or an oboe looks like, and no idea at all of what he must learn in order to play them. This is the gap which this book sets out to fill; firstly to help the reader to make his choice, and secondly to show him how to study the subject of his choice. But before we set about this ambitious task, a word of warning is necessary. You remember the man who was asked whether he could play the piano and replied, " I don't know. I've never tried." If he should buy this book, I can picture him angrily demanding his money back on the grounds that, although he has read every word, he still cannot play the cornet, the harp, or the harmonium. For it must be clearly understood that no book can teach you to play the cornet, the harp, or anything else. But what this book *can* do is to teach you how to teach yourself. It can, as it were, help you to find the cow, provide you with milk-pail and stool, show you how to position your hands. But you, and you alone, can do the milking.

You will have to study, and study earnestly, but if by this you picture hours of drudgery and mechanical repetition of scales and exercises, then let me put your mind at rest right away. Scales and exercises there must be, but modern methods of study have transformed what was once a painful necessity into an interesting and pleasurable pursuit. At last it has been recognised that we must not merely learn to play music ; we must learn to love it as well.

This book does not presume any technical knowledge of music on your part. Even if you cannot read a note of music you will be able to understand it, for though some musical examples are included, they are in no way an essential part of the text. But before you can study an instrument you will have to learn certain rudiments of music, such as the names of the notes and rests, and the various time signatures. For you cannot expect to read until you have mastered the alphabet. These rudiments are included in Chapter III.

The chapters in this book deal with a variety of subjects. You need not study them in the order in which they are written, but it is suggested that you should start by reading the first four chapters. After that, read the other chapters in any order that takes your fancy. The principles outlined in Chapter X (How to Practise) are clearly applicable to any practical subject which you may choose for study, and you should read them very carefully. For knowing *how* to practise is the secret of success.

Finally, do not be put off by any of those theorists and " clever " amateurs who find pleasure in posing as musical intellectuals, and spend their time trying to convince themselves, and others, that music is something obscure and highly complicated, the prerogative of the genius and the connoisseur. Music, more than any other art, is the heritage of simple folk, for it fills one of their greatest needs, the need for relaxation. They have only to enter the realm of music, and all the cares and heartaches, all the trials and disillusionments of a workaday world are forgotten. So let no one dictate to you what music you ought to like or dislike. Play, sing, and listen to all the music you can, and you will very soon find out what pleases you most. And should you discover that you like all kinds of music, so much the better, for then you will have a tune for every mood.

CONTENTS

CHAPTER   PAGE

       PREFACE v

I. WHAT IS MUSIC? 1

II. FIRST STEPS IN MUSIC 7

III. THE A B C OF MUSIC 20

IV. TRAINING YOUR EAR 51

V. THE ART OF PIANO PLAYING (I) .. 57

VI. THE ART OF PIANO PLAYING (II) .. 74

VII. STRING AND WIND INSTRUMENTS .. 81

VIII. THE ORGAN FAMILY 110

IX. PRACTICAL SINGING 118

X. HOW TO PRACTISE 135

XI. LISTENING AND LEARNING 142

XII. THE RISE OF THE ORCHESTRA 148

XIII. THE ROMANCE OF MUSIC 158

XIV. THE MUSIC OF ENGLAND 172

XV. SUGGESTIONS FOR FURTHER STUDY .. 180

CHAPTER I

WHAT IS MUSIC ?

Are you fond of music ? Presumably you are, or you would not be reading this book. But what exactly is music ? Music, says *The Universal English Dictionary*, is " the art of combining sounds or tones for reproduction by the voice or by various kinds of musical instruments in rhythmical, melodic, and harmonic form so as to affect the emotions." So far, so good. But what is Sound, Rhythm, Melody and Harmony ? Before you start practical work it is well that you should know something of the fundamentals of music, so let us take each in turn.

Sound

If you stamp your foot you are producing sound. If, at the same time, you clap your hands you are combining sounds. But it cannot be said that you are making music, though you may be making rhythm. Sound, then, is of two kinds ; that which is heard as noise, and that which is heard as a musical note. All sound is produced by the vibration of something or other. If you strike one of the lower notes of the piano and watch the string, you will notice that the vibrations make it assume a wavy appearance. You can feel the vibrations easily enough by touching the string lightly with the finger. As soon as the pressure becomes heavy enough to stop the vibrations, the sound will cease.

The vibrations of the string, or of whatever body is put in motion, set up, in turn, vibrations of the ear drum, and these cause the sensation of sound. If the vibrations are regular the result is a musical sound ; if they are irregular the result is an unmusical sound. The human ear is sensitive to only a small range of vibrations, and if the ear drum vibrates too slowly or too quickly, the sound becomes inaudible. That is why such sounds as the high notes of a bat's screech are, mercifully, unheard by human ears, though they are probably audible to those animals which have more sensitive hearing, such as the dog. The range of human hearing varies greatly. It is well known, for instance, that the chirp of the cricket, which most people can hear plainly, is inaudible to some whose hearing is normal in other respects.

Musical sound has three characteristics:

(*a*) Pitch (Height or Depth)

(*b*) Power (Loudness or Softness)

(*c*) Quality (the effect upon the ear)

You probably remember the annoyance, when playing a record on an old gramophone which was insufficiently wound, of finding that it was running down. As the music got slower and slower the rousing march which you were enjoying became a funeral dirge. A turn or two of the handle, and the record regained its proper speed, and the march became stirring once more. What had really happened was that the pitch of the music, which had dropped as the record slowed down, had been restored to its proper level. The pitch of a sound is determined by the number of vibrations by which it is produced. When we speak of one sound being higher in pitch than another, we mean that the vibrations producing the higher sound are more rapid than those producing the lower sound. And when we speak of "concert pitch," we mean the standard of pitch which has been adopted by professional musicians in this country. You have probably noticed that, before an orchestra starts to play, one of the players (the oboe in a large orchestra, the piano in a small one) sounds a note, to which the other players tune their instruments. This tuning-up is necessary to make sure that the pitch of all the instruments is identical ; if it were not, they would sound out of tune with one another. Some people possess the faculty of naming, without hesitation, any note played, or of singing any note asked for. Such people are said to have a sense of absolute pitch. Some musicians possess this sense to such a remarkable degree that they are able to name not only musical sounds, but the note of a pig's squeak, or of a clap of thunder.

The power of sound depends upon the length of the vibrations of the sounding body. A pendulum which is swinging slowly over a small space may be made to swing faster over a greater space, and still move backwards and forwards the same number of times a minute. Similarly, a string or other body may be made to vibrate over a wide or narrow space, and the wider the space, the louder the sound will be. The drummer at the rehearsal of the village band who, when requested to play softly replied, " Softly be blowed ! I've come here to enjoy myself," might have produced the pianissimo which the conductor desired had he beaten his drum less vigorously. On the piano, a louder sound is obtained by striking a key sharply than by striking it gently.

A note played on the piano, the violin, the flute or the cornet will produce a different effect on each instrument, even though the pitch, duration, and intensity are constant. This characteristic quality of a sound is called *timbre*, or tone-colour, and full use is made of it when music is arranged for the orchestra. A passage first played on a flute may be taken up by an oboe and then by a clarinet, and though it is repeated three times, the contrast of tone-colour will save it from becoming monotonous. Players of certain instruments are able to vary the quality of the sound ; the violinist may bow or pluck his strings, the trumpet player may play with or without a mute ; and each effect will be quite different.

Rhythm

" In the beginning was rhythm " said Hans von Bulow, and it is perfectly true that very little can exist without it. The leaves fall from the trees, the ducks swim on the village pond, autumn turns to winter, all in rhythm. Rhythm is the heart-beat of music and, as such, music is absolutely dependent on it. Though melody without rhythm would lose its vitality, its strength, and its meaning, rhythm may exist without melody. The simple beating of a drum may rouse a regiment of exhausted men to fresh endeavours.

Rhythm, because it is a sense, is not easy to define, and it is very often confused with time. It is sometimes said that a certain dance orchestra keeps excellent rhythm, when what is really meant is that the speed at which the music is played is regular. If a lively dance tune, such as a jig or reel, were played in strict time, but without a sense of rhythm, it would still lack vitality. And though many people can keep time, fewer can keep rhythm.

Rhythm cannot be taught, but the sense may be developed by practice. Rhythm must be felt physically even if no movement is made. The conductor of an orchestra must first feel the rhythm of the music, before he can convey it to the orchestra by his gestures.

Melody

Melody is often defined as a succession of simple sounds arranged in a pleasing manner. But as it is doubtful whether all melody in modern music is *pleasing*, it would probably be more accurate to substitute *effective*. We cannot say when melody came into being, or whether it existed before speech. Perhaps it found its origin in the first song of the first bird. It is a remarkable thought that although the musical scale contains only twelve notes, the variety of ways in which the composer may arrange them is seemingly inexhaustible. Many melodies are, of course, very reminiscent of one another, and one composer's musical material is often borrowed by another composer ; yet melodies are still being written which are completely original in conception.

When two or more melodies are fitted together simultaneously, so as to form an effective whole, the result is called " counterpoint," or " polyphony." In some compositions one melody is imitated by another melody beginning later at a different pitch, and continually overlapping the first one. This strict form of counterpoint is called " canon." The old " round " or " catch " is a form of canon. You have probably heard the round *Three Blind Mice* sung by several voices. One voice starts off and sings two bars alone. The second voice then chimes in and is joined two bars later by the third voice. And though each voice is singing a different section of the words and the melody, the parts blend together quite satisfactorily.

Harmony

Two or more sounds of different pitch played together form a chord ; and several chords in succession produce harmony. Simple harmony, such as a hymn tune, is mostly in four parts (treble, alto, tenor and bass). The composer arranges the chords in the sequence which he considers will be most effective, and which will allow each of the parts to move as smoothly as possible. The progression of chords and parts is governed by rules which were strictly observed in the past, but which are treated with greater laxity by modern composers.

The dictionary's definition of music mentions its effect on the emotions. Music does, of course, affect the emotions in different ways. The lullaby of a mother soothes her child into sleep, the music of the bagpipes gladdens the heart of the Scotsman, the war chant of the Indian warrior strikes terror into his enemies. But whatever the emotional effect on the listener, music, by appealing to his feelings, encourages him to feel. At the same time it develops his critical judgment, for much music appeals to the intellect as well as to the emotions. Happiness is the greatest incentive to make music. We sing and whistle the most when we are in a gay and light-hearted mood, or when we experience the ecstasy of being in love. And the birds make their sweetest music in the spring.

CHAPTER II

FIRST STEPS IN MUSIC

Playing or Singing ?

The ability to sing and play has always been recognized as a desirable social accomplishment. In Victorian days it was considered proper for young ladies of good family to play the piano or the harp. And often the family would hold a musical evening to which their friends were invited, and papa, in his tail coat and side whiskers, would play a flute solo, and mama would sing " Oh for the wings of a dove " with daughter Harriet at the piano, and then they would all play together, and everyone would go away well satisfied. Those days are past, but even to-day anyone who is able to play the piano or the violin tolerably well, or to sing a song in a pleasing manner, will find that there is a constant demand on his services.

Assuming, then, that you have decided to learn to make music, two questions must be answered ; should you sing or should you play ; and if you play, what should be your instrument ? (Composition is not included as an alternative, for if you really want to compose, nothing will stop you.)

Singing

Firstly, it may be said that everyone who has a voice ought to learn to sing. For singing is the most natural expression of music, and the singer is provided with an instrument which costs him nothing, which never requires tuning, and which is always ready for use. And singing gives men and women an opportunity to make music together, and fosters the spirit of working

7

as a team. It is also an excellent way of improving the speaking voice, and those whose speech is monotonous or hesitant should remember this. If the vocal organs are normal and healthy (as most are), much may be done to improve the volume, range, and quality of a voice that may at first seem weak and thin. The singer is recommended, wherever possible, to learn to play the piano sufficiently to accompany himself, for this will greatly add to his enjoyment of music.

Choosing an Instrument to Learn

The Piano

The piano is the most popular of all instruments for obvious reasons. The music which it produces is complete and satisfying in itself, and it is easier to play than most of the other instruments. The string player and, to some extent, the wind player, has to make his own notes and is therefore liable to play out of tune. The pianist is not concerned with intonation, for his notes are made for him, and he cannot possibly play out of tune unless the piano itself is incorrectly tuned. The pianist, of course, should have a good musical ear, otherwise his playing will be as mechanical as type-writing, and he will scarcely be conscious of what he is doing. But the violinist with a faulty ear will be able to make far less progress. The piano, then, will probably be the choice of many of the readers of this book. And if they are reasonably musical, and really keen to learn all they can about their instrument, they ought to make first-rate progress. No one can promise that they will become virtuosi, for this depends upon their musical and personal qualities, but at least they should attain a degree of proficiency which will enable them to play for their own enjoyment, and that of their friends.

To become an expert performer on any instrument,

it is necessary to take at least a few lessons from an experienced teacher, but if no teacher is available it is quite possible to attain a reasonable degree of proficiency on the piano from a tutor alone.

Some people maintain that long fingers are an enormous advantage to the pianist or violinist. While there is probably some truth in this, the converse does not necessarily apply. People with very short fat fingers may not find it easy to stretch them sufficiently when playing large intervals, but this difficulty may nearly always be overcome by intelligent and assiduous practice.

The Violin

The violin has been called the King of Instruments and, in the hands of a fine player, it is certainly worthy of the name. As a solo instrument, accompanied by the piano, it is well-known for its expressive beauty : it leads the string quartet, and it is the most important instrument in the orchestra. The main difficulty of violin playing, apart from that of keeping in tune, is the acquisition of a fine tone. This demands perfect control of the bow and of the fingers of the left hand, and is only to be attained by much practice and experience. In all matters of tone the ear plays an important part, and the performer, if he is to make real progress, must himself be his severest critic.

Other String Instruments

The technique of the violin applies, to a great extent, to the viola and 'cello, and the standard of difficulty is about the same. The viola is simply a large violin with a tone less brilliant but richer. Its one disability (a slight one) is that it is too small in relation to its pitch. The reason for this is a practical one, for the viola, like the violin, is held between the chin and the shoulder, and if it were made larger it would be too long and heavy to hold up, It would also be too short and small to grip between the knees like a 'cello. The viola is invaluable in the orchestra and the string quartet, but as a solo instrument it is not quite so useful as the violin and the 'cello.

The 'cello has a very full and rich tone, and in the orchestra it is given many solo passages of characteristic beauty. The double-bass, the deepest voiced member of the string family, is primarily an orchestral instrument and is easier to play than the violin or the 'cello, but because of its great size and weight, and the fact that it cannot be used to play solos in the home, it is unlikely to be considered as a possible choice.

Woodwind Instruments

The finger technique of wind instruments is much less difficult than that of the piano or the violin, but the use of the lips, the teeth and the breath must be considered. Certain slight physical disabilities may complicate the playing of wind instruments; missing or irregular teeth may make tone production difficult; respiratory troubles may prevent proper control of the breath. Wind instruments may conveniently be divided into two groups; woodwind and brass. The classification, by the way, is not strictly accurate, for sometimes woodwind instruments are made of metal, and brass instruments of other metals.

There are four kinds of instruments in the woodwind group; flute, oboe, clarinet, and bassoon. Each has a big brother or a little sister. The piccolo is a small flute; the "cor anglais," or English horn, is a large oboe; the bass clarinet is a large clarinet; the double-bassoon a is large bassoon. The flute, oboe, and clarinet are all about the same length, between 2 feet and 2 feet 3 inches; the piccolo measures about a foot, and the bassoon about 5 feet. Of these instruments the flute and the clarinet are the easiest to play, the clarinet probably winning by a short head.

The sound of all wind instruments is produced by making a column of air vibrate in a tube. This is done in several ways. The flautist blows across (not into) a small hole at one end of his flute. The clarinettist has a mouthpiece to which a flat piece of cane (called a reed) is fastened so as to leave a small gap. The player makes the reed vibrate by the pressure of his lips and breath. The oboe or bassoon player's mouthpiece consists of two small pieces of cane bound together with a gap in between. This is called a double reed. The breath must be passed through it slowly and evenly, and the control required to do this makes the oboe and the bassoon two of the most difficult wind instruments to play.

The flute has a brilliant tone, and is extremely agile. The tone of the oboe is penetrating and has a rather nasal quality, but in the hands of a fine player it is very beautiful, and capable of great expression. The clarinet has a smooth, melodious tone. The bassoon is reedy and powerful, and is essentially an orchestral instrument.

The saxophone, found most frequently in the dance orchestra and the military band, is made of metal, but has a reed and mouthpiece similar to those of the clarinet, and is fingered much like the oboe.

The recorder, the old type of flute recently revived, is very suitable for amateur music-making.

Brass Instruments

The group of brass instruments used in the orchestra comprises the French horn, the trumpet, the trombone, and the tuba. The cornet, which is used in brass and military bands, is similar to the trumpet, but it is shorter, has a mellower tone, and is easier to play. The tone of all brass instruments is produced by the action of the player's lips, which take the place of reeds. The horn, which has a coiled tube twelve feet long, is the most difficult to play. The trumpet and the trombone may be heard any day in the dance orchestra, but this style of playing is quite different from that used in the symphony orchestra. The tuba is a large, unwieldy instrument, with a deep, powerful tone.

The Organ

This fine and noble instrument, though by no means easy to play, should not be beyond the capabilities of the keen musical amateur. One difficulty, of course, is that opportunities to practise will be limited, for you can hardly instal a full-size organ in your home. Your best plan is to approach the organist of your local church. He may be able to arrange for you to use the organ for a few hours a week.

Although the technique of the organ differs, in many respects, from that of the piano, the two instruments have a good deal in common. Most people will probably find it easier, and more convenient, to study the piano for a while before trying their hand at the organ. This will especially apply to those whose time for study is limited. The beginner at the organ has many practical difficulties to contend with, and if he knows nothing he may well be overwhelmed by the mass of stops and pedals and keyboards. But if he has some knowledge of the piano they will seem much less formidable.

The fundamental differences between piano and organ technique are as follows :

(1) If the pianist strikes a key and then holds down the sustaining pedal (often miscalled the " loud " pedal),

the sound will continue for a time, even though the hands are lifted from the keyboard. On the organ, the sound is sustained only so long as the key is held down; if the key is raised, it ceases instantly.

(2) When a piano key is struck, the sound decreases in intensity until it dies away. But the power of an organ note remains constant, however long it is sustained.

(3) The pianist can produce various kinds of tone by striking the keys in different ways; if he strikes them sharply the sound will be louder than if he strikes them gently, and so on. But however the organ keys are struck the sound will be the same. The organist can increase or diminish it by other methods, such as the opening and closing of a box-like contrivance which is called a "swell."

(4) The piano has only one keyboard. The organ has two, three, or more keyboards. A group of organ pipes is linked up with each set of these keyboards. The pipes are divided into sets, each set producing a different kind of tone-colour. By manipulating knobs or levers called "stops," the organist is able to use any set of pipes on its own, or several sets in combination.

(5) The pedals of the piano are used simply to sustain or to soften the sound. The organ pedals form an additional keyboard which is played with the feet, and which produces the bass notes, so that the organist has to think of his feet as much as his hands. It may be mentioned that a pedal-board, called a "pedalier," is sometimes attached to a piano, as a means of practising organ music at home.

The Harmonium, American Organ and Electronic Organ

The harmonium and the American organ, either of which may serve as a useful preliminary to organ playing, may be treated together. Both are similar in general construction. The American organ is easier to play, and is more organ-like in sound; the harmonium has greater power of expression and variety of tone-colour. The harmonium has only one keyboard, with a pair of foot-bellows to provide wind. Some of the larger American organs are often electrically driven.

Though not so common nowadays, the harmonium and American organ are very suitable for home music-making. They may often be bought fairly cheaply second-hand, occupy only a small space, and are rather easier to play than the piano.

In the electronic organ the sounds, instead of coming from vibrating reeds, are built up directly from oscill-ating electric currents. The smallest electronic organ (no more difficult to play than the piano) costs about £200; larger models from £300 to £5,000.

The Child Performer

Although it is possible for an adult to pick up at least an elementary knowledge of piano playing from a tutor alone, the average child cannot be expected to make much progress by himself. The earliest age at which music lessons may usefully begin depends upon: (a) the aptitude of the child, and (b) the instrument chosen. The indications of musical talent in young children are often unmistakable. A child may show evident signs of pleasure when listening to music, and the ability to sing or whistle tunes he has heard. Or he may, on his own initiative, try to pick out little melodies on the piano with one finger. Though it is not possible to lay down hard and fast rules, it may be useful to give the approximate age at which a musical child may begin to study an instrument.

The Piano

A child of five, or even younger, may be taught to pick out notes and melodies on the piano, and regular lessons may be begun at the age of seven or eight. A good teacher, using one of the attractive modern piano tutors for young people, can make piano lessons a pleasant game, instead of a dull and boring affair. If a professional teacher is not available, an intelligent adult with a slight knowledge of piano playing could teach a child a good deal with the aid of a tutor, and could greatly help by supervising the child's practice.

String and Wind Instruments

Violins and 'cellos are made in several small sizes for children, and lessons, either individual or in a class, can usually be taken at about six or seven years of age. The viola, being heavier than the violin, is more fatiguing to hold up, and the fingers must also be stretched wider; the best age to start is about fourteen or fifteen, and up to that time the violin may usefully be studied. The double-bass, though the easiest of the string family to master, requires strength which is unlikely to be found in anyone under sixteen.

Of the wood-wind instruments the flute and the clarinet are the easiest to learn, and lessons may be begun at about twelve years of age. The oboe, which is considerably more difficult for a child to play, may be studied at about the same age; the study of the bassoon, a heavy instrument requiring a good deal of wind, should not usually be begun until about sixteen or eighteen.

A child of twelve with normal constitution could quite well begin to study the cornet or the trumpet; work on the French horn or the trombone, which are heavier to hold, should usually be begun rather later.

Practice on any brass instrument is fatiguing to the beginner, and should be limited to a few minutes at a time.

If lessons can be obtained from an experienced teacher, the study of the harp may be begun at about eight years. A child harpist should be tall and of good physique, and should have a sensitive ear.

The Organ Family

It is usually advisable to delay the study of the pipe organ, harmonium, American organ, and electronic organ until some progress has been made with the piano; in most cases fifteen or sixteen is early enough to begin. A child who wishes to study the organ must be tall enough to reach the pedals comfortably.

Final Considerations

You should now be able to estimate, with a reasonable degree of accuracy, the relative difficulty and usefulness of the various instruments. But you may feel that you would like to have more detailed information about a certain instrument—the 'cello for instance. If you know an amateur or professional 'cellist, he will probably be very willing to show you his instrument, to demonstrate its tone, and discuss the various points of technique. Failing this, do not be afraid of approaching one of the 'cellists in your local orchestra, or any professional 'cellist whom you may come across. The end of a concert may provide you with an opportunity to walk up and exchange a few words with him. If he sees that you are genuinely interested, he will probably be quite pleased to tell you what you want to know, and perhaps give you some valuable advice as well.

Apart from the difficulty and usefulness of an

instrument, there are other considerations which may influence your final choice. One of these is the probable cost.

It is not easy to give exact estimates, for values change, but some general indications will help you. It is possible to buy a piano for as little as ten pounds.[1] But it is hardly possible (unless you strike a lucky bargain) to buy a good piano for this price. A secondhand upright piano which is in good order will probably cost you eighty pounds or more, and a small grand piano, or a new upright, may cost you at least two hundred pounds. It is, of course, easier and better to learn to play on a good instrument, and you should buy the best that you can afford. But if it should be the ten pound piano, remember that many brilliant pianists have learned to play on indifferent instruments. (Handel taught himself to play on a broken-down instrument which he smuggled into an attic.)

A violin, complete with bow and case, may be bought for a few pounds or so. Or you may buy a Stradivarius for several thousand pounds. And between the two you may choose an instrument at any price you care to pay. But if you choose wisely, you should be able to buy a sound instrument with a good tone for between thirty and fifty pounds. A viola will be about the same price, and a 'cello rather more expensive.

When you are buying a violin, viola, or 'cello, be sure to choose one which is the right size for you, for sizes vary. Adults, and children over twelve, if they are tall, usually play on a full-size violin, although some ladies prefer a seven-eighth size, which is less tiring to hold up. A three-quarter size is generally used by children of between nine and eleven, and smaller children use half or quarter sizes.

[1]The prices (1971) given in this chapter are only intended to serve as an approximate guide.

Wind instruments, as a rule, are fairly expensive. Approximate prices of new instruments are; flute £50-£200; oboe £160-£200; clarinet £40-£130; bassoon £200; trumpet £30-£75; trombone £35-£100. Secondhand instruments may, of course, be considerably cheaper. But though a cheap violin may possibly be good enough to learn on, this cannot usually be said of cheap wind instruments. Before buying a wind instrument you should be absolutely certain (1) that it is in perfect working order; (2) that it is a modern instrument, of a system that is in general use today[1]; (3) that it is standard pitch (see page 52). If it is any other pitch, or if the system is obsolete, have nothing to do with it.

Another point which you may well consider is portability. The man in the popular song may have taken his harp to a party, but you will not want to carry your harp, or your double-bass, or even, perhaps, your 'cello farther than you can help. And your piano must certainly be considered a fixture. On the other hand, the violin, the viola, and most of the wind instruments, are readily carried about.

One other point worth considering is the attitude of the neighbours towards your practice. Here common-sense must be your guide. If you live in a small block of flats, the occasional practice of scales and exercises on the piano or the violin may not provoke comment. But the trombone or the cornet may not prove so fortunate a choice.

Making a Start

Before you can read music you must learn the rudiments which are contained in the next chapter. You are recommended to spend some time on these, for if you master them thoroughly at the beginning, it will save

[1]See page 99.

you much trouble in the end. But there is no reason why you should not start practical work right away. In this book you will find chapters on piano playing, string and wind instruments, the organ family, and singing. Read the chapter that applies to you.

Whatever the time at your disposal, work to a time-table. Half an hour's practice every day is worth more than six hours' practice once a week. And although you will naturally want to make as rapid progress as possible, do not try to push the pace too fast. If the foundations are not well laid, you cannot hope to build a sound technique. Your motto must be, "Do one thing at a time, and do it thoroughly."

CHAPTER III

THE A B C OF MUSIC

These are the rudiments about which you have been warned. You should spend some time over this chapter, and make certain that you thoroughly understand it. It is arranged in numbered sections, so that it will be easy for you to refer back to any particular section which you may have forgotten.

How Pitch is Represented

1. By the use of signs it is possible to represent both the pitch and the duration of sounds.

2. The pitch of musical sounds is shown by little oval characters, called **notes**, on lines and in spaces ; these notes are named after the first seven letters of the alphabet, A, B, C, D, E, F, G.

3. All the sounds produced by average male and female voices may be represented on eleven lines and ten spaces. These form the **Great Stave**.

4. The names of the notes on the lines of the Great Stave (starting from the lowest line and counting upwards) are G, B, D, F, A, C, E, G, B, D, F.

The names of the notes in the spaces are A, C, E, G, B, D, F, A, C, E.

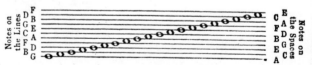

Notice (a) that the lines and spaces follow each other in alphabetical order, and (b) that each line or space is three letters (i.e. a 3rd) above the line or space next below it.

5. In order to make the lines and spaces on the Great Stave easier to read, they are divided into two smaller staves of five lines each. When the note on the middle (6th) line of the Great Stave is required it is introduced on a short line and is termed **middle C.** (For the position of middle C on the piano keyboard, see page 63).

6. The two smaller staves are distinguished from one another by the use of signs called **Clefs.**

7. The two clefs used in piano and organ music are called the **Treble Clef** and the **Bass Clef.**

Normally the treble clef is used for the upper stave (played by the right hand), and the bass clef for the lower stave (played by the left hand). When certain notes are either too high or too low to be written conveniently in the usual clef, however, the clefs are sometimes temporarily interchanged, the right hand playing in the bass clef, or the left hand in the treble clef.

8. The clef is placed at the beginning of the stave, and shows the name of a note on one of the lines of that Stave ; the treble clef is placed on the G line, and the bass clef on the F line.

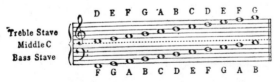

Notice that in addition to the notes on the lines and

in the spaces, a note may be placed above each stave and another below.

9. When sounds above or below the compass of the stave are to be written, short lines called **leger lines** are added temporarily to the stave.

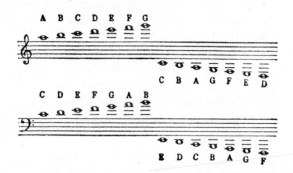

10. We have seen that only seven letter names are used, and if the series of notes is to be continued, it is necessary to repeat the letter names thus :

A B C D E F G, A B C D E F G, A B C D E F G.

Any two letter names which are eight notes apart (A–A, B–B, or C–C) constitute an **octave**.

11. When the sign **8ve** is placed above a note, it means that the note is to be played an octave higher. When the sign **8ve** or **8va bassa** is placed below a note, it means that the note is to be played an octave lower. (These signs are used in very high or very low passages, to avoid using a large number of leger lines. which are often difficult to read).

When the figure **8**, or the words **Con 8va** are placed below a note, the written note and the note an octave below it must be played together.

Sharps and Flats

12. The distance of pitch from a line (or space) to the space (or line) next above or below it is not in all cases equal. The distance between the notes A and B, C and D, D and E, F and G, and G and A, amounts to what is called a *tone* ; whereas the notes B and C, and E and F, are only a **semitone** (or half-tone) apart. The semitone is the smallest division of pitch which is recognized in modern music.

13. It is sometimes necessary to raise the pitch of a note a semitone, by placing a ♯ (called a **sharp**) before it ; similarly a note may be lowered a semitone by placing a ♭ (called a **flat**) before it.

When it is desired to restore a note (which has been raised or lowered a semitone by the addition of a sharp or a flat) to its original pitch, a ♮ (**natural**) is placed before it.

14. On the piano the white keys are called naturals because they represent natural notes (i.e. notes with a simple letter name, A, B, C, and so on) ; the black keys are called sharps and flats because they represent notes raised or lowered a semitone by signs, A sharp, B flat, and so on.

Thus the sound of a sharp is produced from the

black key next above any white key, and the sound of a
flat from the black key next below any white key; for
example, the black key next above the C natural white
key is called C sharp, the black key next below the D
natural white key is called D flat, and so on.

As there is no black key between the natural white
keys B and C, and E and F, however (these keys being a
semitone apart), B sharp is virtually the same note as
C natural, and F flat as E natural. Consequently one
white key does duty for two notes, B sharp and C
natural, C flat and B natural, and so on.

15. It is sometimes necessary to raise the pitch of a
natural note a tone by placing a × (**double-sharp**)
before it, or to lower it a tone by placing a ♭♭ (**double-
flat**) before it.

On the piano (except for B–C and E–F) the sound
of a double-sharp is produced from the white key next
above, and the sound of a double-flat from the white
key next below, the white key representing the natural
note. Thus C double-sharp is represented by the white
key D natural, D double-flat by the white key C natural,
and so on. As the natural keys B and C, and E and F,
are a semitone apart, however, for B double-sharp and
E double-sharp we play the black keys C sharp and
F sharp, and for C double-flat and F double-flat the
black keys B flat and E flat.

16. A double-sharp or a double-flat note is usually
restored to its original pitch by placing a ♮♮ (**double-
natural**) before it, though a single natural (♮) is sometimes used.

The sign ♮♯ placed before a double-sharp note
changes its pitch to that of a single-sharp note, and ♮♭
before a double-flat note changes its pitch to that of a
single-flat note.

17. Every sound may be represented by three different letter names (except G sharp, to which there is only one alternative). If, for instance, the note D is lowered a semitone by placing a flat before it, and the note C is raised a semitone by placing a sharp before it, the pitch of the two notes becomes the same. Here is a chart showing how the same sounds may be differently expressed :

C	C♯	D	D♯	E	F	F♯	G	G♯	A	A♯	B
B♯	D♭	E♭♭	E♭	F♭	E♯	G♭	A♭♭	A♭	B♭♭	B♭	C♭
D♭♭	B×C×	F♭♭	D×G♭♭	E×	F×		G×	C♭♭	A×		

These sounds are said to be the **enharmonics** of one another.

18. When one or more sharps, or one or more flats, are placed *immediately* after the clef, they affect every note on the lines and spaces on which they are placed, and are called the **key signature** of the music. As an example, one may see an F sharp in the key signature written on the fifth line of the treble clef or the fourth line of the bass clef. This means that every F, no matter at what pitch it occurs, will be played as an F sharp.

19. When a sharp or flat, or a double-sharp or double-flat, occurs during the course of a movement, it is called an **accidental,** and affects only the note before which it is placed, and any notes of the same pitch which are included in the bar (for explanation of bar see section 30).

The C Clefs

20. We have seen that the Great Stave consists of eleven lines, of which the five highest form the Treble Clef, and the five lowest the Bass Clef. These two clefs are said to be " fixed," because they always occupy the

B

same position on the stave (see section 8). It is possible, however, to select five consecutive lines from the Great Stave other than those of the Treble and Bass Clefs, which will more conveniently represent the sounds of voices and instruments of medium pitch. When this is done a clef known as the **C Clef** is used, which is said to be " movable," because it may be placed in more than one position on the stave.

21. The C clef is placed on the stave in such a way that it indicates the position of middle C. There are five kinds of C clefs, two of which, the **Alto** and **Tenor,** are in use to-day. The other three are obsolete, but are sometimes found in old music. The relation between the C clefs and the Treble and Bass clefs is shown below.

22. In the following example, a passage is written in the Treble, Bass, Alto, and Tenor clefs ; the effect in each case is precisely the same.

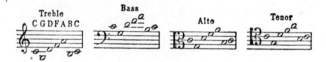

How the Duration of Sound is Represented

23. Different kinds of notes are used to show the length of any particular sound in relation to any other sound. In modern music there are six varieties : **semibreve, minim, crotchet, quaver, semiquaver,** and

demisemiquaver. The table below shows the shape of each kind of note, and its value in relation to the others.

English Names — American Names

A Semibreve — Whole Note

is equal to **2** Minims — Half Notes

or **4** Crochets — Quarter Notes

or **8** Quavers — 8th Notes

or **16** Semiquavers — 16th Notes

or **32** Demisemiquavers — 32nd Notes

24. **A dot** placed after a note increases its value by one half. Two dots increase its value by three-quarters.

$\circ\cdot$ is equal to $\circ$ plus $\downarrow$

$\circ\cdots$ is equal to $\circ$ plus $\downarrow$ plus $\downarrow$

$\circ\cdot$ is equal to $\downarrow$ plus $\downarrow$

$\circ\cdots$ is equal to $\downarrow$ plus $\downarrow$ plus $\downarrow$

$\downarrow\cdot$ is equal to $\downarrow$ plus $\downarrow$

$\downarrow\cdots$ is equal to $\downarrow$ plus $\downarrow$ plus $\downarrow$

25. The sign $\frown_3$ (called a **Triplet**), placed over a group of three equal notes, means that they are to be performed in the same time as two notes of similar value. For example, $\widehat{3}$ equals $\downarrow\cdot$.

When, in piano music, a triplet in one hand is

written against two ordinary notes in the other, the second of the two notes must be played *between* the second and third notes of the triplet.

26. In the same way a **Quadruplet** ⁀4 over four equal notes, means that they are to be performed in the same time as three notes of similar value.

A **Quintuplet** ⁀5 over five equal notes, means that they are to be performed in the same time as four notes of similar value.

Other combinations occasionally met with are the **Duplet** ⁀2 (two notes in the time of three), the **Sextolet** ⁀6 (six notes in the time of four), and the **Septolet** ⁀7 (seven notes in the time of four—or sometimes of six).

Rests

27. Silence in music is indicated by means of signs called **rests,** each equivalent in value to a note. The signs for the rests are:

𝄻 A semibreve rest
𝄼 A minim rest
𝄽 A crotchet rest
𝄾 A quaver rest
𝄿 A semiquaver rest
𝅀 A demisemiquaver rest

Notice that the semibreve rest hangs from the line, but that the minim rest is placed on the line.

28. A dot placed after a rest increases its value by one-half; two dots increase its value by three-quarters.

29. A **pause** 𝄐 placed over or under a note or rest indicates that it is to be prolonged; the duration of the pause is left to the discretion of the performer.

Sometimes the words **lunga pausa** (long pause) are added, when the pause is intended to be of fairly long duration.

How Time and Accents are shown

30. One of the characteristics of melody (and of poetry) is the regular recurrence of strong and weak **accents** or **beats,** which divide it into rhythmic units. In music these units are called **Bars** or **Measures.**

31. The value of a bar is found by counting the number of beats it contains. Thus, if we count four crotchets in a bar, a crotchet would be a beat; if we count three quavers in a bar, a quaver would be a beat, and so on. A beat may be divided into smaller combinations of notes—a crotchet beat may consist of a dotted quaver and a semiquaver, and so on.

32. The position of the strong accent is shown by drawing a perpendicular line across the stave. This is called a **Bar-Line.** The strong accent falls on the beat immediately after the bar-line.

33. Two bar-lines placed together are called **Double Bar-Lines,** and are used to mark the end of a movement or phrase.

34. There are three kinds of bars or measures. **Duple** measure means that each bar may be divided into two equal beats; **Triple** measure into three equal beats; **Quadruple** measure into four equal beats.

35. The kind of bar which has been chosen by the composer for the particular movement, is shown by figures placed on the stave, directly after the key signature. These figures are called a **Time Signature.** Whenever the value of the bars is changed, the time signature must also be changed.

36. If each beat has the value of an *undotted* note, and is therefore divisible into two parts, the music is said to be in **Simple Time.** If each beat has the value of a *dotted* note, and is therefore divisible into three parts, the music is said to be in **Compound Time.**

37. The various time signatures are given below. In the simple times the upper figure shows the number of beats in a bar, and the lower figure the value of the beats; 3/4, for example, means that there are three quarter notes (or crotchets) in a bar; 2/8 that there are two eighth notes (or quavers), and so on. In the compound times the lower figure shows the **divisions** of the beats, the beats being dotted notes of double the value of the lower figure. Thus in 6/8 time the total value of the bar is equal to six quavers, but the actual beats are dotted crotchets (i.e. double the value of quavers), two of which are equal to six undotted quavers.

Table of Time Signatures.

		SIMPLE TIMES		COMPOUND TIMES	
	Time Signature	Value of one bar		Time Signature	Value of one bar
DUPLE	¢ or 2/2	♩ ♩		6/4	♩. ♩.
	2/4	♩ ♩		6/8	♩. ♩.
	2/8	♪ ♪		6/16	♪. ♪.
TRIPLE	3/2	♩ ♩ ♩		9/4	♩. ♩. ♩.
	3/4	♩ ♩ ♩		9/8	♩. ♩. ♩.
	3/8	♪ ♪ ♪		9/16	♪. ♪. ♪.
QUADRUPLE	¢ or 4/2	♩ ♩ ♩ ♩		12/4	♩. ♩. ♩. ♩.
	C or 4/4	♩ ♩ ♩ ♩		12/8	♩. ♩. ♩. ♩.
	4/8	♪ ♪ ♪ ♪		12/16	♪. ♪. ♪. ♪.

38. A bar may consist entirely of notes or rests, or partly of notes and partly of rests, so long as it is of the exact value indicated in the time signature.

Syncopation and Phrasing Marks

39. **Syncopation** is the displacement of a regular accent, so that it falls on a part of the bar not usually accented, as in the following example :

The example below shows two different ways of effecting syncopation.

" Carneval "   Schumann, Op. 9.

(a) In bars one and three an accented note is placed on an unaccented beat. The altered accent is frequently marked with a stress (>) as in this example. (b) In bars two and four a note on an unaccented beat is tied (see section 40) to one on an accented beat.

40. It will be noticed that in the first of the above examples the E's are joined by a short curved line ⌢. This is called a **tie.** When two or more notes of *similar* pitch are tied together in this way, the first note must be sustained for the length of all the notes, and the tied notes must not be sounded.

41. When a curved line (similar in shape to the tie) is placed over or under two or more notes of *different*

pitch, it is called a **slur.** In instrumental music the slur indicates that the notes under it are to be played as smoothly as possible. In vocal music the slur is frequently used when two or more notes are to be sung to one syllable.

42. A dot placed over or under a note is called a **staccato mark,** and means that the note is to be short and crisp.

A dash means that it is to be still shorter.

A dot with a slur over it means that the note is to be not quite so short as when the dot is used alone.

Intervals

43. An **Interval** is the distance, or difference in pitch, between any two sounds. The smallest interval in modern music is the semitone.

44. Semitones are of two kinds. (*a*) A semitone which is formed by two notes having different letter names (B to C, E to F, and so on) is called **Diatonic,** a word meaning " through the tones, or degrees, of the scale." (*b*) A semitone which is formed by two notes having the same letter name (C to C sharp, D to D sharp, and so on) is called **Chromatic,** which literally means " coloured " ; in a figurative sense a note may be looked upon as coloured when it is raised or lowered in pitch by means of an accidental.

45. The size of an interval may be calculated by counting the letter names upwards, from the lower note to the higher note, both notes being included in the total ; C to D is a second, C to E a third, C to F a fourth, and so on.

46. The quality of an interval may be **perfect, major, minor, diminished** and **augmented.**

47. Any interval which is counted from the first note of a major scale to any other note of that scale, must be either major or perfect.

In addition to the perfect intervals of a fourth, fifth and octave, the **unison,** which is formed by two notes of the same pitch and letter name, is spoken of as perfect, though strictly speaking it is not an interval at all. The unison is shown thus :

48. If a major interval is reduced by a semitone, **by** flattening the upper note or sharpening the lower **note,** it becomes a minor interval. Thus, C to E is a major third, but C to E flat and C sharp to E are minor thirds.

49. If a perfect or a major interval is increased by a semitone, by sharpening the upper note or flattening the lower note, it becomes an augmented interval. Thus, C to D is a major second, but C to D sharp and C flat to D are augmented seconds.

50. If a perfect or a minor interval is reduced by a semitone, by flattening the upper note or sharpening the lower note, it becomes a diminished interval. Thus, C to G is a perfect fifth, but C to G flat and C sharp to G are diminished fifths.

51. An interval may be **inverted** by placing either

the top note an octave lower, or the bottom note an octave higher. Perfect intervals, when inverted, remain perfect ; minor intervals become major ; major intervals become minor ; augmented intervals become diminished, and diminished intervals become augmented.

52. An interval which does not exceed the compass of an octave is said to be **simple ;** one which does exceed it is said to be **compound.** A compound interval is a simple interval to which an octave has been added ; a compound interval may be reduced to a simple interval by subtracting seven. Thus, a ninth (9—7=2) may be reduced to a second, a tenth (10—7=3) to a third, and so on.

53. Intervals which appeal to the ear as complete in themselves, and do not require another sound to follow, are said to be **consonant ;** intervals which leave a sense of incompleteness, and a desire for resolution into some other sound, are said to be **dissonant.** The intervals usually classed as consonant are all perfect intervals, and major and minor thirds and sixths ; those classed as dissonant are major and minor seconds and sevenths, and all augmented and diminished intervals.

Play the two intervals below and you will notice that the first (a dissonant augmented fourth) sounds incomplete until it is resolved into the second (a consonant minor sixth), which gives an impression of completeness.

Scales and Key Signatures

54. **A scale** is a series of sounds arranged in alphabetical order to form an octave.

55. There are two kinds of scales in modern use : **Diatonic** and **Chromatic.** The diatonic scale consists of tones and semitones ; the chromatic scale entirely of semitones.

56. There are two kinds of diatonic scales, **Major** and **Minor ;** each consists of seven different notes, each note being placed in or on a different space or line.

If the scale is continued beyond the seventh note, the eighth note will be a repetition of the first note at a different pitch, the ninth note a repetition of the second note, and so on (see section 10). Although the diatonic scale is made up of only seven *different* notes, the ear does not recognise it as complete until the eighth note (the octave) is added.

57. The major scale consists of tones and semitones arranged according to a definite plan ; the interval of a semitone occurs between the 3rd and 4th, and 7th and 8th degrees (i.e. notes), and that of a tone between the other degrees.

58. The major scale of C is called the **natural** scale because it is constructed entirely from natural notes (on the piano only the white keys are used).

SCALE OF C MAJOR

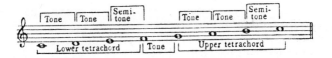

From the above example you will see that the major scale is divided into two halves or **Tetrachords** (a Greek word originally applied to the four strings of the lyre). Each tetrachord consists of precisely similar intervals—two tones followed by one semitone. The two tetrachords are separated by the interval of a tone.

59. Every major scale is constructed according to this pattern. If we take the upper tetrachord of the scale of C major, and add a tetrachord above it, we form an entirely new scale.

SCALE OF G MAJOR

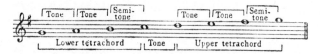

You will see that the first degree (also called the **key-note**) of the new scale is G ; that is, the fifth note of the scale of C major. To make the upper tetrachord conform to the regular pattern—tone, tone, semitone—the third degree of the tetrachord (i.e. the seventh degree of the scale) must be raised a semitone.

In the scale of G major (which takes its name from the key-note, G), therefore, the seventh degree (F) is sharpened. This sharp, which is obviously vital to the construction of the scale, is placed at the beginning of the stave, immediately after the clef sign, and is known as the **key-signature.**

60. A key-signature may consist of either sharps or flats (from one to seven), and these are known as **essentials** because they affect every note of the same letter name throughout the movement. Thus they differ

from accidentals (see section 19), which affect notes of
the same pitch and letter name only in the actual bar in
which they occur.

61. By taking the upper tetrachord of the scale of
G major, and adding a tetrachord above it, we may form
the scale of D major. (Notice that the key-note is again
the fifth degree of the old scale).

SCALE OF D MAJOR

To make the upper tetrachord conform to pattern,
the seventh degree of the scale must be raised a semitone,
by adding another sharp to the signature.

62. By continuing this process we may form,
successively, the major scales of A, E, B, F sharp, and
C sharp. Each time the fifth degree of the old scale
becomes the key-note of the new one, and the seventh
degree of the new scale is raised a semitone by adding
a sharp to the key-signature.

SCALE OF A MAJOR

SCALE OF E MAJOR

SCALE OF B MAJOR

SCALE OF F SHARP MAJOR

SCALE OF C SHARP MAJOR

63. If we take the lower tetrachord of the scale of C major, and add a tetrachord below it, we form the scale of F major, the first of the series of major scales having one or more flats in the key-signature.

SCALE OF F MAJOR

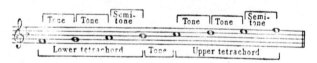

Notice (a) that the key-note of the old scale now becomes the fifth degree of the new one ; and (b) that in order to obtain a semitone between the third and fourth degrees, and a tone between the two tetrachords, the fourth degree of the new scale must be lowered a semitone, by giving the scale a key-signature of one flat.

64. By continuing this process we may form,

successively, the major scales of B flat, E flat, A flat, D flat, G flat and C flat,[1] each time lowering the fourth degree of the new scale by adding another flat to the key-signature.

SCALE OF B FLAT MAJOR

SCALE OF E FLAT MAJOR

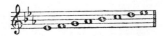

SCALE OF A FLAT MAJOR

SCALE OF D FLAT MAJOR

SCALE OF G FLAT MAJOR

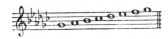

[1] When memorising the order of the major keys it should be noted that the names of the flat keys are those of the sharp keys reversed.

SCALE OF C FLAT MAJOR

65. The minor scale is so named because the interval from the key-note to the third degree is minor (see section 48). The earliest form of minor scale comes from the scale system of the ancient Greeks, and is one of the old Church scales or **modes**—the Aeolian.

SCALE OF A MINOR—ANCIENT FORM

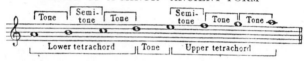

This scale, like that of C major, is formed of natural notes, and there is an interval of a tone between the seventh and eighth degrees. In order to produce a semitone between these degrees (one of the features of our modern scalic system), the ancient form is usually modified in modern use.

66. If we sharpen the seventh degree of the ancient minor scale, we form what is known as the **harmonic minor scale.**

SCALE OF A MINOR—HARMONIC FORM

By sharpening the seventh degree of the scale, the interval between the sixth and seventh degrees becomes an augmented second (a tone-and-a-half). This interval was forbidden in old music, which was mostly for voices, because it was considered difficult to sing. With the rise of instrumental music the harmonic minor scale found favour, and is now the form most used in modern music.

67. In order to overcome the objection to an interval of an augmented second between the sixth and seventh degrees, the **melodic minor scale** was evolved. Its peculiarity is that the sixth and seventh degrees are sharpened in ascending, and restored to their original pitch in descending.

SCALE OF A MINOR—MELODIC FORM

68. Since the harmonic and melodic forms of the scale of A minor are evolved from the ancient form, which is composed of natural notes and has no sharps or flats in the key-signature, the seventh degree of the harmonic scale, and the sixth and seventh degrees of the melodic scale, are regarded as being accidentally sharpened ; this means that the sharps are used as accidentals, instead of being inserted in the key-signature. Similarly, the naturals in the melodic scale of A minor (descending) are used as accidentals.

69. Since the ancient scale of A minor and the scale of C major are both formed from natural notes, and neither has sharps or flats in the key-signature, A minor is spoken of as the **relative minor** of C major, and C major as the **relative major** of A minor.

From the natural scale of A minor a series of minor scales may be constructed which is relative to the series of major scales formed from the natural scale of C major. Major and minor scales which are relative to one another have the same key-signature, the sixth degree of the major scale being the key-note of its relative minor.

70. The process of forming major scales has already been described, and much the same process applies to the formation of minor scales. To form the " sharp " series we take the upper tetrachord of a scale and add a tetrachord above it ; to form the " flat " series we take the lower tetrachord and add a tetrachord below it. Two points must be noted, however. (1) The two tetrachords which form the minor scale are not identical in construction, like those of the major scale ; the tetrachord which forms the basis of the new scale must therefore be modified. (2) To form the harmonic minor scale the seventh degree must be accidentally sharpened ; to form the melodic minor scale the sixth and seventh degrees must be sharpened in ascending, and restored to their original pitch in descending.

71. To make this process clear let us form the scale of E minor. We take the upper tetrachord of the scale of A minor (ancient form), and above it add a tetrachord consisting of a semitone, a tone, and a tone. Since E is the sixth note of G major, the two scales are relative to one another ; the scale of E minor, therefore, has a key-signature of one sharp. This sharp has the effect of raising the second degree of the scale a semitone or, in other words, of modifying the upper tetrachord of the old scale to make it conform to the lower tetrachord of the new one.

SCALE OF E MINOR—ANCIENT FORM

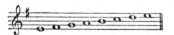

We may now turn the ancient scale into either the harmonic or the melodic form. In the harmonic form the seventh degree is accidentally sharpened.

SCALE OF E MINOR—HARMONIC FORM

In the melodic form the sixth and seventh degrees are accidentally sharpened in ascending, and restored to their original pitch in descending.

72. The remaining minor scales are formed by a similar process. Here are the signatures of the major and relative minor keys. The keys of C flat major and its relative, A flat minor, are rarely used.

MAJOR, AND RELATIVE MINOR KEYS

73. Each degree of a diatonic scale has a technical name. In Tonic Sol-fa a similar system of naming the degrees is used. It should be remembered that the degrees of the scale are always counted upwards.

Degree		Name	Tonic Sol-fa
1st ..	..	**Tonic or Key-note**	DOH
2nd..	..	**Supertonic**	RAY
3rd ..	..	**Mediant**	ME
4th ..	..	**Subdominant**	FAH
5th ..	..	**Dominant**	SOH
6th ..	..	**Submediant**	LAH
7th ..	..	**Leading Note**	TE
8th ..	..	**Tonic or Key-note**	DOH

74. A minor scale whose key-note is the same as that of a major scale is said to be the **tonic minor** of that scale. The key-signature of a minor scale has three sharps less, or three flats more, than that of its tonic major ; C sharp major, for instance, has seven sharps, and C sharp minor four ; E flat major has three flats, and E flat minor six.

75. The chromatic scale, consisting of semitones only, contains twelve different notes arranged in alphabetical order : there may be two notes of the same letter name, however ; C and C sharp, D and D flat, and so on. It is usually formed by taking the notes of the major scale and filling in the missing semitones, sharpening the notes in ascending, and flattening them in descending. The white-headed notes in the example below are those of the major scale, and the black-headed notes those added to form the chromatic scale.

Signs, Abbreviations and Ornaments.

76. Two or four dots placed on the left of a double bar mean that the preceding movement is to be repeated.

Placed on the right of a double bar they mean that the movement which follows is to be repeated.

77. The words **1ma Volta** or **1st Time,** and **2da Volta** or **2nd Time** are often printed over bars where a repetition occurs. They mean that the bar or bars marked 1st Time are to be left out when the movement is repeated, and the bar or bars marked 2nd Time performed instead.

78. The sign **D.C.** or **Da capo** means that the music is to be repeated from the beginning of the movement.

The sign **D.S.** or **Dal Segno** means that the music is to be repeated from the sign $.

79. The word **Fine** (the end) is sometimes placed over a double bar to mark the conclusion of the piece.

80. A silent bar is indicated by a semibreve rest; several bars silence is indicated by a rest with a number placed over it.

81. The word **bis** (twice) written over a bar means that it is to be played twice.

82. The **Appoggiatura,** or leaning note, is a small note written before the principal note, and taking half its value, if it is an undotted note, and two-thirds of its value, if it is a dotted note. It is only found in old music; modern composers give the note its proper written value.

Written   *Performed*

83. The **Acciaccatura,** or crushing note, is written like the appoggiatura, but with a stroke through the stem. It is sounded on the beat as quickly as possible before the principal note, but it does not receive the accent.

84. The **Upper Mordent** is indicated by the sign ～

placed over a note, and consists of three notes, the principal note, the note above it, and the principal note, performed in rapid succession.

Written   Performed

85. The **Lower Mordent** is indicated by the sign ∿ placed over a note, and is performed in the same way as the Upper Mordent, except that the three notes consist of the principal note, the note below it, and the principal note.

86. The **Turn,** or **Gruppetto,** is indicated by the sign ∽ placed over or after a note, and consists of a figure of four notes, the note above, the note itself, the note below, and the note itself. This figure is performed either instead of, or after, the note itself.

Written   Performed

Written   Performed

87. The **Inverted Turn,** indicated by one of three signs ∾ , ∫, or ⌘, and placed over or after a note, is performed in the same way as the turn, except that the figure of four notes consists of the note below, the note itself, the note above, and the note itself.

88. The **Shake,** or **Trill,** indicated by the sign **tr.** or **tr.** ‿‿‿, consists of the rapid alternation of the written note and the note above it. The Shake usually ends with a turn.

Written   Performed

89. In piano music, the notes of a chord are sometimes played in rapid succession from the bottom upwards, each note being held as it is played. Chords played in this way are said to be **spread** or played as an **arpeggio.** The effect is indicated in either of two ways:

Musical Terms

Most of the terms denoting speed, expression, and intensity of sound are written in Italian. The following list contains the principal terms in general use.

Accelerando (accel.)	Quickening the tempo
Adagio	Leisurely
Affettuoso	Tender
Affrettando (affret.)	Hastening
Agitato	Agitated
Allargando (allarg.)	Enlarging, broadening.
Allegretto	Animated, but not so fast as **Allegro**
Allegro	Lively, cheerful
Amoroso	Lovingly
Andante	At a moderate pace; not so slow as **Adagio**
Andantino	Quicker than **Andante,** though employed by some composers to indicate a slower tempo
Animato	Animated
Appassionata	Passionately
A poco a poco	Gradually
Assai	Very
A tempo	In time (after **rall.** or **accel.**)
Attacca	Go on, attack

Ben Marcato	Well marked
Bravura	Spirit, dash
Brillante	Brilliant
Calando	Decreasing in volume or speed, or both
Calcando	Hurrying the time
Cantabile	In a singing style
Colla voce	With the voice
Con brio	With vivacity, spirit
Con espressione	With expression
Con fuoco	With passion
Con moto	With animation
Crescendo (cres. or <)	Becoming louder
Deciso	With decision
Decrescendo (decres. or >)	Becoming softer
Delicato	Delicate, gentle
Diminuendo (dim.)	Becoming softer
Dolce	Sweet
Espressivo	With expression
Forte (f.)	Loud, strong
Fortissimo (ff)	Very loud
Fortepiano (fp)	Loud, them immediately soft
Furioso	Impetuously
Giocoso	Joyful
Grandioso	Grand, magnificent
Grave	Solemn—also used to indicate a tempo which is slower than **Adagio**
Grazioso	Graceful
Incalzando	Increasing in speed (and force)

Larghetto	Slow, but faster than **Largo**
Largo	Broad, slow
Lentamente	Slowly
Lento	Slow
L'istesso tempo	The same time
Lusingando	Caressingly
Ma	But
Maestoso	Majestic
Mancando	Waning in tone
Marcato	Marked
Martellato	Hammered
Meno	Less
Mezzo-forte (mf)	Moderately loud
Mezzo-piano (mp)	Moderately soft
Moderato	At moderate speed
Molto	Much; very
Morendo	Dying away
Non troppo	Not too much
Pastorale	In a pastoral style
Perdendosi	Dying away
Pesante	Heavily
Piano (p)	Soft
Pianissimo (pp)	Very soft
Più mosso	With more movement
Poco a poco	Little by little
Prestissimo	Very quick
Presto	Quick, nimble
Rallentando (rall.)	Gradually becoming slower
Ritardando (ritard.)	Gradually becoming slower
Ritenuto (rit.)	Held back
Scherzando	Playfully
Sempre	Always

Sforzando or	
Sforzato (sf. or sfz.)	Accented, marked
Simile	In the same manner
Smorzando	Extinguishing (the sound)
Sostenuto	Sustained
Sotto voce	In a subdued manner
Strepitoso	Boisterously
Stringendo	Quickening the tempo
Tacet	Be silent
Tempo commodo	In convenient time
Tempo primo (Tempo. 1.)	The first (original) time
Tempo rubato	Lit. "in robbed time", i.e. a time in which one part of a bar is played slower or faster at the expense of the other part
Tenuto (ten.)	Held, sustained
Tranquillo	Tranquil
Tutti	All (the parts or performers)
Vigoroso	Vigorously
Vivace	Lively, brisk
Vivo	With vivacity
Volta Subito (v.s.)	Turn over quickly

CHAPTER IV

TRAINING YOUR EAR

Music is a word that is frequently misused. Many people speak of music as if it were synonymous with the piano. So that although Willie's father pays a considerable sum for his son's *music* lessons, all that young Willie really learns is to play a couple of simple pieces on the piano, to the delight of his parents, and to the discomfiture of everybody else.

Just as the artist or the sculptor uses his eyes, so the musician uses his ears, as much as, or more than, his hands, and a musician who is totally deaf is as handicapped as an artist who is blind. Yet a great many amateur players appear to be deaf to the music which they are trying to play, which, as a result, becomes meaningless, and a travesty of something which might have been beautiful. So if you would be a musician in the real sense of the word, a musical artist who feels what he hears and hears what he feels, you must train your ear as carefully as your fingers, so that you will be able to pass critical judgment on everything that you play yourself, and hear others play.

You may have a natural ear for music, in which case you will be able to develop it very easily. But if you feel that you have only a very poor ear at the moment you should not be dismayed, for it may be improved, by practice, to a remarkable degree.

A Simple Method of Ear-training

Here is an easy way to develop your sense of pitch. You must first purchase from your music dealer either a tuning-fork (sometimes called a pitch-fork) or a pitch-pipe. It will cost you only a small sum. A tuning-fork is a small metal fork shaped like this:

If the fork is held by the handle (marked A), and one of the prongs (marked B) is struck against something hard, the prongs will vibrate. The sound may be heard either by bringing the fork close to the ear, or by applying the end of the handle to a solid surface, such as the top of a piano or table. A pitch-pipe is a little pipe about two inches long, which produces a note when blown. Ask for a fork or pipe in C, and make certain that it is international standard pitch (a′ = 440). Make the fork or pipe your constant companion for the next few weeks or months. Whenever you have an opportunity, strike the fork, listen carefully to the note, and hum it. As soon as you can do this easily and accurately, you can proceed to the next stage. This time try to hum the note *before* you strike the fork; then listen to the fork, and hum the correct note. Your first attempts will probably be very wide of the mark, but if you persevere you will find that before long you can pitch the note with tolerable accuracy.

If you have a piano you can, of course, strike the note C, instead of using the fork or pipe. But this is not nearly so convenient, for you cannot slip your piano into your pocket, or take it to bed with you.

When you can pitch the note of the fork correctly and easily, you will be able to invent other exercises for yourself. Here is one suggestion. Listen to the note of the fork (C), and then hum the note a third higher (E). Next time, hum the note *before* striking the fork. Then do the same with the note a fourth higher than the fork (F), and so on. You should frequently vary the exercises by *thinking* the note instead of actually humming it : this will teach you to hear music with your mind as well as with your ears.

A sense of absolute pitch,[1] though to some extent a natural gift, can often be developed by practice on these lines—orchestral musicians and conductors frequently acquire it from the constant association of certain sounds with a fixed pitch. This " tone-memory " usually brings with it an aptitude for learning music by heart ; it is also a valuable aid to the performance of unaccompanied vocal music. The possession of a sense of absolute pitch may have its disadvantages, however; when, for example, a piano is of a pitch other than that to which the performer is accustomed, he may be disconcerted to find that he is playing music in one key and hearing it in another.

Practice at the Piano

If you can play simple pieces on the piano, you can use them to practise ear-training. We shall take as an example a very simple tune " Drink to me only with thine eyes," but hundreds of other tunes would serve equally well. Start by clapping, or tapping with a pencil, the rhythm of the tune. This is what you will clap :

Next play the tune right through on the piano, being very careful to keep strict time. Then play bars 1 to 4, and clap the rhythm of bars 5 to 8 ; continue playing bars 9 to 12, and clap the rhythm of bars 13 to 16. Next time reverse the process ; clap the rhythm of the first four bars and play the next four bars, and so on. Do this with other songs, hymn tunes, and simple piano pieces. You will find it an enjoyable way of developing your sense of rhythm.

Practice away from the Piano

In addition to practising with the tuning-fork, you should try to develop your sense of rhythm and melody as much as you can.

You will find clapping or tapping rhythms very helpful. Another useful exercise to improve your sense of rhythm is stepping and clapping. In this exercise, you step one rhythm and clap another. You may, for instance, clap twice as fast as you step, or you may step twice as fast as you clap. As a variation of stepping and clapping, you may tap a different rhythm with each hand. You will find this much more difficult, for you will have to overcome the natural tendency of the hands to move together.

The melody line of most songs and hymn tunes will provide material for sight-reading. Start with some simple melodies in the key of C major, and gradually work through the more difficult keys. If you have an opportunity of practising with a friend you should seize it, for it will be most helpful. One of you can test and correct the other, and you will both be encouraged to make rapid progress.

Playing by Ear

Many people, some of whom have received no

musical training, possess the gift of playing by ear. They are able to reproduce on the piano a song or piece which they have heard on the radio or at the cinema, although the reproduction is seldom an accurate one.

If they also have a natural feeling for melody and harmony, they may be able to invent simple tunes at the piano. In its higher branches this is called improvisation, or musical composition at the keyboard. In its more elementary forms it is largely a matter of musical memory, and the quality of the reproduction depends upon the accuracy with which the music is retained. It will generally be found that the amateur player is only able to use a very few chords, and to play in two or three simple keys. Although playing by ear is a useful accomplishment, and is worth developing on sound lines, the beginner at the piano may actually find it a handicap. For when he starts to read simple piano music, he may find that he is improvising his own harmonies, instead of playing what the composer has written. If he continues to do this, he may eventually find it almost impossible to play printed music correctly. This state of affairs may be avoided if, in the early stages, the pianist is aware of his failing, and deliberately stops and restarts each time he finds himself " improving " on the composer's ideas.

Exercises in Ear-training

The following example is intended to be used in several ways :

(1) Clap or tap the rhythm of the top line.
(2) Sing the top line.
(3) Clap the rhythm of the bottom line.
(4) Sing the bottom line.
(5) Sing the top line, and clap the rhythm of the bottom line.

(6) Sing the bottom line, and clap the rhythm of the
    top line.
(7) Play the top line on the piano, and sing the
    bottom line.
(8) Play the bottom line on the piano, and sing the
    top line.

Stepping and Clapping

Each of the exercises should be repeated several
times, and should be used as follows :

(1) Clap the top line, and step the bottom line.
(2) Step the top line, and clap the bottom line.

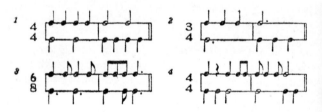

Now try to invent similar exercises yourself.

CHAPTER V

THE ART OF PIANO PLAYING (I)

The Music of the Piano

The piano possesses a repertory greater than that of any other instrument. There is probably no piece of music of any kind which has achieved popularity, which may not be purchased as a piano arrangement. And though the piano is a mechanical instrument—next to the organ it is the most mechanical of all instruments—it is a medium for which the greatest composers have ever delighted to write.

Most of the great composers themselves started as pianists: Mozart, Haydn, Beethoven, Mendelssohn, Schumann, and Chopin, to name a few. So the richest musical treasures, the Preludes and Fugues of Bach, the Sonatas of Beethoven, the Valses and Nocturnes of Chopin, are to be found amongst piano music. In addition, there is a vast collection of lighter pieces with which we may amuse ourselves whenever we wish. Surely, in this great library, there is music for every taste, and for every mood.

Early Keyboard Instruments

The piano as we know it to-day, is a comparatively modern instrument, but we may trace its origin at least as far back as the beginning of the fifteenth century. Each of the earliest keyboard instruments, the clavichord, the virginal, the spinet, and the harpsichord, contributed something to the modern piano. There is no conclusive evidence as to which of these instruments was the first, though the clavichord, on account of the simplicity of its construction, would seem to be the most likely.

The clavichord is usually in the form of a box without legs, which may be placed upon a table for playing. The action of the keys is simple and direct. When a key is depressed, a slender strip of brass, which is attached to it, is brought in contact with the string, and sets it in vibration. The action of the virginal and spinet, and of the harpsichord, is quite different, for the strings are plucked by means of quills, or points of leather. The harpsichord is sometimes fitted with two or three keyboards, acting on different sets of strings, and occasionally it has stops like those of an organ. By means of these it is possible to obtain some variety of expression.

Compared with the modern piano, the early keyboard instruments sound extremely weak, and they have little power of sustaining tone. Their sweet, gentle voices are best appreciated if heard in a small room. During the seventeenth and eighteenth centuries, harpsichord making developed into a fine art, and many elegant instruments were constructed, some as large as the modern grand piano. The harpsichord became the favourite instrument of the fashionable young ladies of the period, who, apparently, were sometimes more beautiful than musical. For Samuel Pepys, a great lover of music, records in his diary of 1663 that he "went to hear Mrs. Turner's daughter play on the harpsichord; but, Lord! it was enough to make any man sick to hear her; yet I was forced to commend her highly."

In recent years, there has been a revival of interest in the harpsichord and clavichord. Modern and improved instruments are available for the performance of old and new music. A new harpsichord or clavichord may cost from £200 to £1,750 according to size.

The Story of the Piano

The piano is commonly said to have been invented by an Italian called Cristofori, in 1709, but it is by no means certain that pianos did not exist before then. Nevertheless, the keyboard mechanism which Cristofori introduced undoubtedly laid the foundations of the modern piano action. Cristofori's mechanism was ingenious. The felt-covered hammers which struck the strings were independent of the keys, and were lifted to the strings by pieces of wood called " hoppers "; a device called an " escapement " allowed the hammers to fall immediately from the strings, leaving them free to vibrate. There was also a system of dampers, which were raised when the keys were depressed, but which fell as soon as the fingers were lifted, bringing the sound to an end. These principles, with certain modifications, apply to the piano action of to-day.

Cristofori called his pianos *gravicembalo col piano e forte*—literally, a harpsichord with soft and loud—from which we get the word pianoforte. The piano passed through a long experimental period. At first it had no pedals, and the power of sustaining tone was very limited. Sometimes levers were added, which were controlled by the knees, and produced a *forte* effect by raising the dampers from the strings (like the sustaining pedal of a modern piano), and a *piano* effect by introducing a thin strip of cloth between the hammers and the strings. When pedals made their appearance they were used for many purposes, some of them strange. One variety of cabinet piano, which was more than six feet high, and looked rather like a grand piano stood on end, had no less than six pedals. One of these was known as the " bassoon," and brought a strip of parchment in contact with the strings; another pedal operated a drumstick which hit the belly of the instrument; a third struck some bells ; and there were two kinds of soft pedals and a damper pedal.

The piano frame was at first made of wood, but this was not found to be strong enough to withstand the enormous tension, and the frame was later reinforced with, or built entirely of, metal. The strings, which because of their thinness were difficult to keep in tune, were made thicker, and, as a result, the tension was increased, and to-day, in the largest grand pianos, it is often as much as thirty tons.

The compass of the piano was also extended by gradual growth. Of the two pianos by Cristofori that still remain, one has four octaves and the other four-and-a-half ; but the compass of the modern piano is usually seven or seven-and-a-quarter octaves. So the weak sounding spinet and clavichord grew into an instrument of expressive beauty, and a marvel of mechanical ingenuity.

How to Master the Piano

No one has yet discovered a royal road to piano playing, or, for that matter, to golf and tennis. Certain principles may be laid down in each case : the golfer, for instance, may be shown how to hold his club, and how to swing it ; and he may be warned to keep his eye on the ball. But that ease of movement, that control of head and hands on which his game depends, is not to be gained except by patient and careful practice. And if, in his eagerness, he hurries any particular process unduly, he will find his muscles stiffening up, and his stroke becoming jerky and ineffective.

It is the same with piano playing. The pianist must start on the right lines, and continue on those lines ; and each time he finds himself stiffening up, or doing anything else which is clearly wrong, he must stop and make a fresh start. For nothing is harder to break than a bad habit which has been persevered in.

One of the most important things that the pianist has to learn is how to practise. That is why a later chapter has been entirely devoted to it. But for the moment we are concerned with the basic principles of piano playing, of which it will be assumed that you know nothing.

Your Position at the Keyboard

You should sit in the middle of the piano on a stool rather than on a chair, but if you use a chair you must be careful to sit forward and not to lean against the back. You should sit at such a distance from the keyboard that when your arms are naturally bent, your fingers will fall easily upon the keys, and your feet reach comfortably to the pedals. The seat should be of such a height that your elbows are on about the same level as the keys. Your elbows, by the way, should not be raised ; they should hang loosely and naturally, fairly close to the body.

Your hands should be arched, not flat ; imagine that you are clasping an orange in each hand, and they will assume the correct positions. And as most of your playing will be done by the tips of the fingers, the nails should be kept short.

Modern Methods of Study

Piano technique has undergone many changes during the last hundred years. Innumerable theories have been advanced and methods of study devised, which have found favour for a time, and have then been superseded by fresh ideas. Exercises for strengthening and conditioning the fingers, to be performed away from the piano, have been advocated from time to time, and mechanical appliances have even been made for this purpose. Schumann invented a contrivance for holding back the third finger of his hand, so that he might attain greater dexterity with the others ; as a result he lost the use of his finger, and with it his hopes of becoming a great pianist.

Liszt, one of the world's greatest pianists, was responsible for many changes. He encouraged his pupils to sit much higher at the piano than was usual at the time, so that the hands could be brought down with greater force on the keyboard. Though Liszt himself never abused his power, he was responsible for a school of pianists whose chief aim was to get every ounce of available tone from the piano, often breaking hammers and strings in the process. When this brutal treatment of the piano had run its course, a more gentle method of tone production was advocated.

Ideas have changed, too, about the action of the wrist and arm. For a long time it was held that the wrist must remain completely still, the fingers only making any movement. Moscheles, the great pianist and teacher, even suggested to his pupils that they ought to be able to play with a glass of water balanced on each wrist. Nowadays, both the wrist and the arm are allowed free movement.

The Piano Keyboard.

Here is a diagram of a section of the piano keyboard. You will see that there are eight white notes and five black notes to each octave (C to C), and that between the notes E and F, and B and C, there is no black note ; they are therefore a semitone apart. Any two white notes which have a black note between them are always a tone apart.

What you must know about Touch

Press down any white key on the piano, with the middle finger of your right hand. Now raise the finger, letting the key come up again. Notice that if the key is pressed down as far as it will go, it will come to rest on a soft, yielding surface. This is called the " bed " of the key. You must always press the key right down until it reaches the bed, otherwise the note may not sound.

Now put your right hand thumb on the middle C key, that is, the C key in the middle of the piano, and nearest the lower end of the lock. Starting on middle C, and using your fingers in order, play five consecutive white keys, so that when you reach the fifth note you land on your little finger. Now come down again. What you have played is called a five finger exercise. Play it several times, and watch your fingers carefully. They should be at right angles to the keyboard, and they should not be pushed so far forward that the black keys get in their way. About an inch of the thumb should rest on the key ; the other fingers will fall naturally into position.

If you play the five finger exercise quickly, you will find that it is not possible to raise the fingers very high, and you need not try to do so. In very quick and light passages the fingers need not leave the surface of the keys. In passages that are not so quick, the weight of the hand and finger exertion will help to produce the tone. And where the fullest, roundest tone is wanted, the weight of the forearm, or of the whole arm, may be used. But you must make certain that there is no drive behind the fingers, and that the tone is produced simply by the weight of the arm and hand falling on the keys. You should practise letting the arm fall limply to the side of the body, as if it were a dead weight. Then, keeping the arm just as limp, raise it above the keyboard and let it drop on to the keys. If the arm is raised in this way, the fingers will fall naturally into a cup-like position, and the hand will drop down, as if it were on a hinge. Remember that this hinge should work easily ; there must never be the slightest sign of stiffness or tension.

You see, then, that the way to develop a good tone is not to *strike* the keys, but to use the exertion of the fingers and weight of the arm. Rigidity of any part of the body must be avoided at all costs, for it is likely to produce jerky movements, and a hard tone. And remember that your ear is the best judge of good tone ; so make it work full time.

What you must know about Pedalling

The modern piano has two pedals ; the one on the right is the damper, or sustaining pedal ; the one on the left is the soft pedal. (A third pedal is usually fitted to pianos made in the United States and Canada, but it is hardly ever found in this country, and we need not concern ourselves with it).

If you examine the inside of a piano, you will see the dampers, made of wood and felt, resting on all the strings except the shortest ones. (The shortest strings have very little power of sustaining tone, so they do not need dampers). You will also see that the lowest notes have either one or two strings each, and that the other notes have three strings each. When you depress a key, the damper attached to that key is raised, to allow the strings to vibrate. When the key is released, the damper returns to the strings, and stops the vibration and the sound.

When the damper pedal is depressed, it raises all the dampers from the strings, so that any notes which have been sounded continue to sound even though the keys are released. The sound is sustained until the dampers are lowered, or until the vibrations of the strings come to an end. The use of the damper pedal also *enriches* the sound, for when one string is set in vibration with the dampers raised, all the other strings are free to vibrate in sympathy with it.

Although the damper pedal makes possible many effects which could not be produced without its aid, it is also a potential source of danger. For unless it is used with caution, it may easily ruin what might otherwise be considered good playing. Many pianists do not understand how and when to use the damper pedal. As a result, they are either afraid to use it at all, or they use it in the wrong places, with the result that all the music that they play sounds muddy, with the notes and chords running into one another. This is a pity, because the principles of good pedalling are really quite simple.

Some piano music is marked to show where the damper pedal is to be used. The sign " Ped." means that the pedal is to be depressed, and a star shows when it is to be released. But these markings are not always to be relied upon, and in any case there is a great deal of music without them, so that the player must decide for himself where, and where not, to use the pedal.

In pedalling, the heel should not be raised from the floor. When the pedal is not in use, the foot may remain on it, ready for further action. If you are playing a slow succession of chords which you wish to make as smooth as possible, you may pedal each chord. But you must use the pedal in the following way. Play the first chord, wait a moment, and then depress the pedal. Play the second chord, releasing the pedal at exactly the same time. Wait a moment, and then depress the pedal. Play the third chord, releasing the pedal at exactly the same time. And so on. The pedal must be raised and depressed to its full extent.

As an experiment, play a series of notes or chords, putting down the pedal at the exact moment that you play each note or chord. Listen carefully to the result. Either the notes or chords will run into one another, or the pedal will make hardly any difference at all. The reason is that if the pedal is raised and depressed too quickly, the dampers will not have time to do their work. The first principle of pedalling, then, is to wait for the sound, and then depress the pedal.

The top strings of the piano, having no dampers, are not affected by the pedal. And even those upper strings that have dampers are less effected than the lower strings. You can easily prove this for yourself. It is therefore possible to sustain one or more notes in the bass, by means of the pedal, while playing light scale passages in the treble. But unless these scale passages are fairly high up the result will be blurred. (To prove this, play the five finger exercise already mentioned, starting on middle C, and keeping the pedal down throughout). In this, your ear must be the judge of what is good or bad.

You must change the pedal (if you use it at all) whenever there is a change of harmony in the music. Otherwise the notes, or chords, will run into one another. Your ear will tell you when a change in pedal is necessary. Look at this example :

Surely you would not keep the pedal down during the whole of this passage? Your ear tells you that a change of pedal is necessary between the first and second bars. Your eye also tells you, for it is clear even from the *look* of the music that there is a change of harmony in the second bar. But it would be instructive to play the passage with the pedal down throughout, and then to play it as marked.

There is one more principle of pedalling to consider. Sometimes you will come across a passage where a long note is sustained in the bass, with changing harmonies above it which will not permit of the pedal being held down throughout. Here is an example:

It is clear that the left hand cannot hold down the bass, and at the same time play the moving chords. But the passage may be played by using what is known as half-pedalling. In this pedalling, deliberate advantage is taken of the fact that if the pedal is changed quickly enough, the dampers will not have time to check the vibrations of the strings properly, and the sound, particularly if it is in the bass, will continue. In the passage above, the octave in the bass is played, and the pedal put down. Then, as each of the chords is played, the pedal is raised and depressed with the utmost possible speed, with the result that the bass note continues to sound throughout the bar.

The soft pedal acts in one of two ways. On upright pianos the pedal, when depressed, moves the hammers nearer to the strings ; on grand pianos it moves the keyboard and hammers to one side, so that where there are three strings to a note, only two are hit, and where there are two strings to a note, only one is hit. The depression of the soft pedal is indicated by the words *Una Corda* ; the words *Tre Corde* show that it is to be raised.

The soft pedal should only be used when a certain kind of tone-colour is wanted by the composer ; it should never be used merely to produce soft effects— these must be obtained from the fingers. The soft pedal and the damper pedal are used quite independently ; either may be used alone, or both may be used together.

What you must know about Fingering

Until a few years ago, two systems of fingering existed in this country. Nowadays only the Continental system is used ; in this the thumb is marked 1, and the fingers, in order, 2, 3, 4, 5. The English system, in which the thumb is marked with a +, and the fingers, in order, 1, 2, 3, 4, is sometimes found in old music. You should make certain that any music you buy has Continental fingering.

A great deal of printed music has the fingering marked, and this should generally be followed. But remember that the same fingering may not suit every player ; the printed fingering is intended for average-sized hands, so that if your fingers are very short or very long, you may need to alter it.

Ideas of fingering, like ideas of touch, have changed a good deal in recent years. In the old days, one of the most important principles was that the thumb was not to be used on black notes, except where this was absolutely unavoidable. But in modern fingering the thumb is freely used on black notes. This should be remembered when playing from old editions, which may be fingered in the old-fashioned way. When playing scales and exercises you should always use the printed fingering, for this has been devised with some special purpose in view. Where no fingering is marked, work out the most simple fingering you can ; the easiest is nearly always the best.

How to play Scales and Arpeggios

Scales and arpeggios are the basis of all piano technique. If you look at any piano piece you will realize their importance, for you will find that most of the music is based on some kind of scale or arpeggio figure.

We shall start with a very easy scale ; C. major :

Play the right hand first. Start with the thumb on middle C. Play the next two notes (D and E) with the first and second fingers. Now pass the thumb under the hand, and play the fourth note (F) with it. (You must, of course, hold down the E with the third finger, until you are ready to play the next note with your thumb). Use the next three fingers in order, 2, 3, 4, to play the notes G, A, B, then pass the thumb under the hand, and play C.

You have now played one octave. The next octave is fingered in the same way, but when you reach the top C, play it with your little finger instead of your thumb. Coming down the scale you use the same fingering but in the reverse order ; starting with the little finger, you use the fingers in order for the first five notes, and then you pass the third finger over the thumb, to play the sixth note.

If you look at the fingering for the left hand, you will see that it is the same as that of the right hand in reverse ; the left hand going up is fingered like the right hand coming down, and vice versa.

Practise the scale with each hand separately. Play it quite slowly and softly at first, and listen carefully to what you are playing. Make sure that every note is smooth and regular. Pay particular attention to the passing of the thumb under the hand, and of the second finger over the thumb ; these are the places where the scale is most likely to be uneven.

When you have mastered each hand, play both hands together, in similar, and in contrary motion. In similar motion the hands play an octave apart ; in contrary motion both hands begin on the same note (middle C), and move in opposite directions.

You should memorize the fingering of the C major scale ; you will then be able to play the major scales of G, D, A, E, and B, which are fingered like it. The other scales are fingered on the same principles, but they do not always start with the same fingers. You should buy a book of scales and arpeggios, and follow the fingering exactly. Then learn to play them all from memory.

Arpeggios are sometimes called " broken chords," and this is exactly what they are. The notes of the chord, instead of being struck together, are played one after the other. Here is the arpeggio of the common chord of C major. Study the fingering very carefully.

The secret of arpeggio playing is to let the thumb pass smoothly under the hand, keeping the elbow as still as possible and never jerking it.

Practise a few scales and arpeggios every day, even if only for ten minutes. There is nothing better for improving the technique.

How to Play a Solo

As soon as you are able to read simple music, and have mastered the elementary principles of piano playing, you will want to play a solo. There is a large number of very easy pieces from which you may choose.

When you start to play a piece, you must first of all concentrate on getting the notes right, at the same time making sure that you are using the correct fingering. After this you should play the piece as slowly as you like, but in strict time and rhythm. You will probably find that some passages are comparatively easy, but that others present difficulty. You must play these passages separately, finding out just where the difficulty lies, and practising until you have overcome it. You can then increase the speed of the music by degrees, playing it a little faster each time, until you have reached the proper pace.

You will now be able to turn your attention to the phrasing and expression of the music. The phrasing marks will tell you which passages are to be played smoothly and which are to be played *staccato*; the expression marks will tell you which passages are to be played loudly and which softly, and where the music is to swell or diminish. Take note of any *rallentandos*, *accelerandos*, and pauses. Decide when and when not to use the damper pedal.

Finish by polishing up the piece as a whole. Make certain that the style and mood in which you are playing is the right one. A hornpipe or a country dance demands a different treatment to a funeral march or a lament.

When you have made some progress, and have learned to play several pieces, make a point of going over the earlier and easier ones from time to time. With your added experience you will be able to play them with greater confidence than ever before.

How to make a Start

We have so far dealt with the general principles of piano playing, and with individual points of technique and interpretation. You should refer back to these whenever you come up against a difficulty.

It is now time to draw up a plan of campaign for your study. Your rate of progress will depend on the time you are able to devote to practice, but you should not try to hurry the early stages; each book of exercises or pieces should take you several months to thoroughly master.

From the many good tutors, methods and albums for the piano, you should choose one or two which suit your requirements. Technical exercises and pieces may be studied side by side, and these may be varied from time to time so that constant interest is maintained.

A useful series of exercises dealing with the problems with which the learner is likely to be confronted is *Piano Technique on an Hour a Day* by Geoffrey Tankard and Eric Harrison (Elkin). *Favourites* by Henry Duke (Novello) could go with this; it contains twelve easy pieces. If you wish to teach a child, there are many attractive albums, such as *First Piano Lessons* by May Sarson (Novello).

When the technical exercises have been mastered, you should get *The Hundred Best from Czerny* (Paterson), which is issued in several graded books. Book 1 contains twenty-nine short exercises by Czerny, the great piano teacher and composer of the nineteenth century, whose exercises have been used by countless pianists. You will also need a book of scales and arpeggios; Donald Gray's *Scales and Arpeggios* (Boosey & Hawkes) is suggested.

You should now be able to choose your own solos, which may include some of the easier classics. Nearly all the publishers issue a graded series of piano pieces classified as very easy, easy, moderately difficult, and so on, so that you should have little difficulty in making a suitable choice.

CHAPTER VI

THE ART OF PIANO PLAYING (II)

Accompanying at the Piano

The accompanist has always been thought of in the popular mind as a pianist who is not good enough to play solos. In Victorian days, young ladies who were not particularly musical learnt the piano " sufficiently to play accompaniments."

But though piano accompaniment may not demand quite such a high standard of technical skill as solo playing, there are other important qualifications which are sometimes not found in the solo pianist. The accompanist usually has to play most of his music either at sight, or with the minimum of preparation ; this is no easy matter, and is only to be accomplished by systematic practice in sight-reading. The soloist, on the other hand, has time in which to study and prepare his music ; that is why many indifferent sight-readers are competent solo players. The accompanist, if he is doing his job properly, must follow the tempo and interpretation of the singer or player whom he is accompanying, and must even be prepared to skip a page or so of the music, if the singer's memory should suddenly fail him. The soloist is under none of these obligations ; he can choose his own tempos, and if he wishes to indulge his temperament by leaving out a few pages of the music, or by playing it twice as slowly as it should be played, no one can stop him.

There is another point worth mentioning. The soloist, when he performs before an audience, is generally expected to play from memory, but the accompanist is usually allowed to keep his music in front of him. And it is a curious fact that the majority of pianists are either good sight-readers or good memorizers, but seldom both. Sight-reading and memorizing are dealt with at some length in another chapter. All that has been said about piano technique applies, of course, to the accompanist, but there are other important things which he should know.

It has been said that the accompanist often has to read music at sight, or with little preparation, but it is hardly necessary to mention that he should always practise his music beforehand, if he has the chance. He is far more likely to do justice to music which is familiar than to an unknown piece. The copy from which he plays will be printed on three, and sometimes more, staves. The two staves which are to be played by the piano will be printed in bold type, and bracketed together. If the piece is an instrumental solo, the solo part will be printed in smaller type, and the clef appropriate to the instrument will be used (the treble clef for the violin ; the bass, tenor, or treble clef for the 'cello ; and so on). If it is a song, the vocal line will be printed in the same size type as the piano part, and the words will appear underneath. In addition to playing his own part, the accompanist must follow the solo line, and though it is not always necessary or possible to read every note of this, he must be able to take in the outline of the part in sufficient detail to give the soloist every possible support.

When playing accompaniments to songs, the beginner will find it helpful to follow the words as closely as possible ; then, if he loses his place for a moment, he can quickly find it again. He must be prepared to make his accompaniment an elastic one, and he must not expect the singer to sing everything exactly as it is printed in the music. The singer will often hurry one phrase and pull back another, and if he comes across a note which he likes, he may stay on it for some time. Experience, and a knowledge of human nature, will enable the accompanist to read the singer's mind so faithfully that nothing comes as a surprise.

In the accompaniment of instrumental solos, a rather different technique is required. For here the piano is not necessarily relegated to mere accompaniment, but is often just as important as the solo instrument. If, for instance, the piece is a sonata for violin and piano, the two instruments will be treated as equals, and the piano, in addition to accompanying the violin, will have many solo passages on its own.

Instrumentalists, as a rule, keep more strictly to the tempo and directions printed in the music than vocalists do ; but the accompanist will find that it is easier to lose his place, and more difficult to find it, in instrumental music, where there are no words to guide him. In this, his ear will help him as much as anything.

The accompanist must remember that his principal function is to give the soloist support, and unless the piano part contains something of importance, he must be careful not to play so loudly that he distracts the listener's attention from the soloist. When a deep instrument, such as the 'cello, is to be accompanied, the damper pedal must be used with caution, otherwise the lower sounds of the 'cello may be obscured.

Piano accompaniment is an art which is too often neglected by the amateur ; it is a useful and fascinating branch of music, and well worthy of the most careful study.

Four Hands at one Piano

The playing of piano duets seems to have been more popular during the last two centuries than it is to-day. Special instruments were sometimes constructed for duet-playing. Dr. Burney, who, in 1776, wrote the first important history of music in the English language, and also composed some of the earliest piano duets, says that (I am quoting from the *Oxford Companion to Music*) "the ladies at that time wearing hoops, which kept them at too great a distance from one another, had a harpsichord made by Merlin, expressly for duets, with six octaves."

A considerable number of original works have been written for four hands at one piano, and, in addition, there are many arrangements of famous symphonies, overtures, and chamber works. By writing for four hands, it is possible to compose or transcribe music which could not be effectively played by the solo pianist, and so a large library of pieces is added to the repertory of the piano.

Duet-playing is one of the most enjoyable ways of learning to read piano music at sight. Technically, piano duets are easier to play than solos. And there are many very simple duets suitable for two beginners, the musical effect of which is fuller and more satisfying than that of solos of a similar grade.

The players sit close together in front of the keyboard, sometimes on a long music stool especially made for duet-playing. The left-hand player plays on the lower half of the keyboard, and the right-hand player plays on the upper half ; the music is so arranged that the two parts do not overlap. It will generally be found convenient for the left-hand player to work the soft pedal, and the right-hand player the damper pedal.

The music is printed on one copy, with separate parts for each player. The part on the left-hand page is called the *Secondo* ; the part on the right-hand page is called the *Primo*. This is simply the Italian for " second " and " first." The second part is usually written in the treble and bass clefs, and sometimes the bass clef is used for both hands. The first part, which is often the easier of the two, is usually written in the treble clef for both hands, although the bass clef is occasionally used for the left hand.

The players must decide who is to turn over; usually it is better for the second player to do so. But if either player has a rest in the music at the turn of the page, he should do the turning. The page should be turned over a bar or so before the end, for it is easy to memorize the last bars of each page, but impossible to determine what the first bars of the next page will be until it is turned over.

It is advisable to choose duets which are well within the capabilities of each player, otherwise it may be difficult to keep a steady tempo and rhythm. And to get the greatest benefit and enjoyment, the players should change parts frequently.

Choosing your Piano

The choice of your piano will be determined by the price that you can afford to pay, and whether you want an upright model or a grand. Other things being equal, the tone of an upright is not to be compared with that of a grand. On the other hand, a grand is usually more expensive, and it takes up more room. If you know nothing about pianos, your best course is to go to a first-class firm, who will be able to show you a selection of different instruments.

There are several sizes from which you may choose. The full-size grand is only suitable for a large room, but the boudoir model may be accommodated in any fair-sized room, and the baby and miniature grands take up very little more space than an upright. The largest uprights are sometimes known as " upright grands." These are usually overstrung, which means that the strings are arranged diagonally, one group of strings crossing the other group. This gives additional length to the strings, without increasing the height of the piano. The upright is also made in a small size, known as the cottage piano, which is usually only about four feet high. There are some small pianos in which the strings are replaced by tuning forks, which does away with the necessity of tuning. The tone is weaker than that of an ordinary piano.

If you buy a piano from a secondhand dealer, or at an auction room, without having it examined by an expert, you are taking a big risk. But it will help you to know what points you should look for yourself. You will be able to judge from the general appearance whether the piano has been well looked after. How old do you think it is? Pianos, unlike violins, do *not* improve with age. Try all the keys (not only a few), and see whether they respond instantly, and whether the touch and tone is satisfactory. Try the pedals. Do they work properly? Do they squeak? Look inside at the hammers and the dampers. Are the felts badly worn? If they are, they may have to be renewed, an expensive item. Are there any signs of moth? Is the piano very badly out of tune? If it is, it has probably been neglected for some time.

Looking after your Piano

A really good piano may last you a lifetime if if you look after it. One of the best ways of looking after a piano is to play on it regularly. Then dust and moth will not be so likely to settle in it, and the action should remain in good order.

Closing the piano when you have finished playing will help to keep out dust and damp, but may encourage moth. Choose the position for your piano with care. Do not place it directly under a window, or anywhere in a draught. A position near an inner wall, and a short distance from some form of heating, is best. Damp is the worst enemy, as it may cause rust to form on the strings, and the action to bind.

Above all, have your piano regularly and properly tuned. There are plenty of bad tuners, but few good ones. The best way to get a good tuner is to make a contract with one of the leading piano makers, who will send you one of their tuners at regular intervals. Three times a year will be sufficient. Ask the tuner to keep your piano up to concert pitch. If you have a tuning-fork or a pitch-pipe, you can test the pitch yourself.

If anything should go wrong with the piano, it is usually wiser not to touch the action, but to leave it to an expert. The piano has a delicate inside, and it is quite easy to break a hammer or a damper.

CHAPTER VII

STRING AND WIND INSTRUMENTS

THE VIOLIN

The modern violin, a descendent of the viol family, first came into use in Italy, during the latter part of the sixteenth century. In the city of Cremona, the Amati family, and later the Guarneri and Stradivari families, made violins which, notwithstanding many attempts at improvement during the last two hundred years, have never been surpassed and seldom equalled.

The Cremonese instruments which are still in existence are highly prized, and their tone and construction is considered by connoisseurs to be much finer than that of modern violins. The instruments of Antonio Stradivari (1644–1737) are usually rated highest, because of their wonderfully full, sweet, even tone. The Amati, Guarneri and Stradivari families had many imitators, whose work was sometimes very good, and sometimes indifferent.

Thousands of violins bear the label of some famous maker, but this usually indicates the model which the instrument follows, rather than the name of the maker himself. Genuine Strads and Amatis are not to be picked up for a mere song in some secondhand shop, although good instruments by the lesser makers may sometimes be discovered in unlikely places.

Apart from the Italian violins, there are many fine old instruments by French and English makers. Of the English School, Benjamin Banks (1727–1795) is usually given the foremost place.

Choosing an Instrument

Choosing a violin is no easy task, even for those with some years of experience. Unless you have a friend who is competent to give an opinion, it is best to be guided by a firm of repute. Such a firm will be able to demonstrate the different qualities of various instruments, and will not try to represent an imitation bearing a fictitious label as the genuine work of an old master.

Experts do not always agree upon the extent to which a violin improves with age. Some believe that the tone of a 200-year-old instrument has altered very little since the day it was made. But few will deny that a newly made violin takes a certain length of time to settle down. It may, perhaps, be expected to improve by being played upon for a year or more, after which the tone will remain more or less constant.

The qualities of a violin are largely conditioned by the choice of the wood and varnish, and by the way in which the different pieces (there are over eighty) are fitted together. If twenty new violins by the same maker, of the same kind of wood and varnish, and of exactly similar appearance were tested, one would probably be found to be greatly superior to the others. This is because the wood from which the violins were fashioned, though taken from the same tree, displayed slightly different qualities in each instrument.

The real test of a violin is the tone, which should be sweet, full, and pleasing to the ear, and of a uniform quality throughout its compass. If the tone is satisfactory the appearance is of little consequence, but an instrument which has been badly fractured should be avoided. Small fractures may sometimes be repaired satisfactorily, but the purchase of a fractured violin is decidedly a speculation.

The Violin and the Bow

The Violin consists of a wooden sounding-box, formed by two surfaces called the belly (made of soft wood such as pine) in which two holes, resembling the letter *f*, are cut, and the back (made of hard wood such as sycamore), which are united by the sides or ribs. A neck, ending in a curved scroll, is attached to the sounding box, and an ebony fingerboard is fixed to the neck. The strings, which pass over the belly of the instrument, are fixed at one end to an ebony tail-piece, and at the other end to movable pegs by which the pitch may be raised or lowered. The strings are raised from the belly by a small wooden bridge, which is supported by a little wooden sound-post placed in the interior of the instrument. The bridge is curved, so that the bow may be drawn across each string separately without coming in contact with the others.

The bow consists of the stick, made of hard wood such as Brazilian lance wood or Pernambuco, straight at one end and curved at the other. White horse-hair is attached to the curved end of the stick, and to an ebony head (also called a " nut," or " frog ") which may be made to slide to and fro by turning a metal screw at the straight end of the bow, thus tightening or loosening the hair. The stick of the bow is cut straight, and afterwards bent by subjecting it to heat. This gives the stick a springy quality.

Before playing, the hair of the bow should be adjusted so that it is moderately tight, but not so tight as to pull the stick out of shape, and should be drawn lightly across a stick of resin, to increase the grip. When not in use the hair should be loosened slightly, so as to relieve the stick of any strain.

The hair of the bow, seen under a microscope, has tiny teeth like those of a saw. These teeth wear away after much playing, and must be renewed. The bow should be taken to a competent firm of repairers, for the rehairing needs to be skilfully done. If the bow is used for an hour a day, it will require new hair every three or four months.

The strings of the violin are tuned in perfect fifths thus :

4th String   3rd String   2nd String   1st String

G   D   A   E

Formerly the E, A and D strings were made of gut, and the G string of gut covered with silver or copper wire. Nowadays the E string (and sometimes the A and D strings) are usually made of wire. Though the quality of tone is not to be compared with that of gut strings, wire strings last longer, and keep better in tune. When they are used, a little appliance called a " string adjuster " must be fitted to the tailpiece, because of the difficulty of making fine adjustments with the peg.

Tuning

To tune the violin, sit down, place the left hand round the neck of the instrument, and hold it upright on the knees. Sound the note A, either on the piano, or on a pitch-fork or pipe, and pluck the A string with the thumb of the left hand. Adjust the string by slowly turning the peg with the right hand ; if the string is sharp, turn the peg towards you ; if it is flat, turn the peg away from you. Be sure to press the peg well into its socket as you turn it, to prevent it slipping back. If, in spite of this, the peg slips badly, it is best to treat it with a special soap which is sold for the purpose, afterwards dusting it with chalk. When you have tuned the A string, tune the E string in the same way. To tune the

D and G strings, take the violin into the right hand, and turn the pegs with the left hand.

This method of tuning is easiest for the beginner, but as soon as progress has been made, the violin should be tuned by holding it firmly under the chin, the left hand turning the pegs, while the right hand plays the string with the bow. Start by tuning the A string, and tune the others by sounding two strings together (first A and D, then D and G, and lastly E and A), listening carefully to the perfect fifth so formed, to hear whether it is in tune.

When tuning, take care that the bridge is not pulled forward in the direction of the scroll. If this happens it may fall down, and the little wooden sound-post may then be displaced. This may be avoided by always keeping the bridge very slightly inclined backwards. If anything should happen to the bridge or sound-post, their adjustment should be left to an expert ; the beginner who attempts to position them may do more harm than good.

The Correct Playing Position

The violinist should stand with the left foot slightly forward, the weight of the body resting on it. The violin should rest upon the left collarbone, with the chin, slightly tilted to the left, gently pressing upon the instrument. The position should be such that the player can look straight ahead at the neck of the instrument. The neck should be held between the thumb and fore-finger of the left hand, with pressure just sufficient to prevent it from sinking into the hollow between thumb and finger. The thumb must not protrude too far, or it will prevent the player from using the G string. Here is the correct position of the hand :

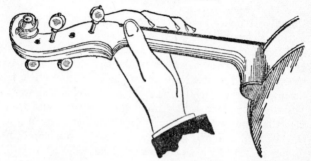

The violin should be held high, and not allowed to drop ; this may be accomplished by bringing the left elbow well under the instrument. The player should be able to support the violin by the chin and collarbone alone, so that if he takes away the left arm, the violin will remain in the correct position. This may be facili-tated by fitting a vulcanite chin-rest, which allows the chin to secure a better grip. Some players use a pad for the shoulder, but this has the effect of deadening the vibration of the instrument, and is not to be recommen-ded. But a silk handkerchief placed over the lapel of a jacket will save wear and shine.

The Use of the Bow

The bow is held lightly between the four fingers and

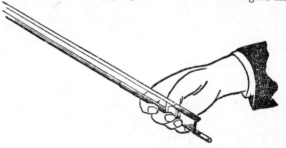

the thumb of the right hand. The thumb is slightly bent, and placed against the stick close to the nut, so that it lies opposite to the middle finger.

The bow must be drawn firmly across the strings, with the stick somewhat inclined towards them, so that the hair is turned towards the bridge. The bow must be drawn in a line parallel with the bridge, and the distance from bow to bridge should usually be about an inch. The nearer the bow is drawn to the bridge, the louder will be the tone ; but the bow should never be so near that the tone becomes harsh.

The stroke of the bow from the heel to the point is called a " down bow " ; that from the point to the heel is called an " up bow."

In the early stages, bowing should be practised before a mirror, and particular attention should be paid to keeping the bow strictly parallel with the bridge. The change from a down bow to an up bow, and vice versa, must be carried out as smoothly as possible ; in the hands of a skilled player it is scarcely perceptible to the ear. The change is made by a movement of the wrist. In a down bow, as the point of the bow is being reached, the wrist gradually turns the stick towards the bridge, turning it back again (that is, towards the fingerboard) as soon as the up bow is started. The change of bow should be practised, using full bows and drawing them as slowly as possible, and listening carefully to the result.

The stroke of the bow may either be changed for each note, or several notes may be played in one stroke. When several notes are played smoothly in one bow, they are said to be " slurred." When each note is given its full value, and the notes follow each other in the smoothest possible manner, they are said to be played with *legato* bowing. The development of legato bowing is important, for it is one of the most useful and charming strokes on the violin. In passing from one string to another, the change must be made by means of the wrist ; if the wrist action is right, the arm will follow naturally.

Another style of bowing often used is the *staccato* stroke. In this stroke, the notes are played in a short, crisp manner, and are separated from one another. The upper half of the bow (the half nearest the point) should be used. Several notes may be played *staccato* in the same stroke, by stopping the bow between each note, without letting it leave the string.

The *martelé* (or hammer) stroke is often used where a strong accent and a firm tone is wanted. This stroke is played at the point of the bow, by pressing the hair firmly on the string, and then playing with a quick, elastic pressure of the wrist.

Fingering

The fingering of all string instruments which are played with a bow (violin, viola, 'cello, and double-bass) is based on the fact that if a string is made shorter, the pitch will be raised. If, then, a string is pressed down on to the fingerboard by one of the fingers, it is shortened, or " stopped " by the finger. A string that is not stopped is said to be " open " ; the use of an open string may be indicated by the sign o placed over (or under) a note. The four fingers of the left hand may be used for stopping notes. The thumb, of course, is not available. The use of the different fingers is shown by the figures 1, 2, 3, or 4 placed over (or under) a note.

If the first finger is pressed down on the 4th (G) string, about an inch up the fingerboard, it will stop the note A ; the second finger placed about an inch from the first will stop the note B ; and the third finger, placed close to the second, will stop the note C. If the fingers are placed in the same position on the 3rd (D) string, they will stop the notes E, F sharp, and G, so that the scale of G major may be fingered thus :

It should be noticed that the second and third fingers are placed closer together than the first and second fingers. The reason for this is that B to C and F sharp to G are semitones, whereas A to B and E to F sharp are whole tones.

If the fingers are placed in the same positions on the 2nd (A) string, they will stop the notes B, C sharp, and D ; on the 1st string (E), they will stop the notes F sharp, G, and A.

So far we have only considered the first three fingers. Now suppose that the fourth finger is pressed down on the G string, about an inch away from the third finger. The note stopped will be D, that is, the same note as the next open string. This means that the note D (above middle C) may be produced either by stopping the G string with the fourth finger, or by playing the open D string. Similarly, the fourth finger on the D string will stop the note A, and the fourth finger on the A string will stop the note E. There is, of course, no open string above the E string ; the fourth finger on it will stop the note B.

When stopping notes, the tips of the fingers of the left hand must be pressed down very firmly on the strings.

We have seen that if the first finger is pressed down on the G string, about an inch up the fingerboard, it will stop the note A. If it is moved back a little so that it is about half an inch up the fingerboard, it will stop G

D

sharp. Any of the fingers may be placed a little farther back, in this way, so as to lower the stopped note by a semitone. Any of the fingers may also be placed a little farther forward, so as to raise the stopped note by a semitone. Thus, if the third finger is placed a little farther forward on the G string, it will stop C sharp, instead of C. In this way, a chromatic series of notes may be played. The following table of fingering should be studied :

G	G sharp	A	A sharp	B	C	C sharp	D
Open G String	1	2	2		3	3	4 or Open D String

It will be seen that by using the fingering so far given, a complete chromatic scale may be played, extending from the open G string to B (fourth finger on the E string). It is possible, however, to extend the upward compass beyond B, and to provide many alternative ways of fingering on all the strings, by moving the hand up the neck of the violin (towards the bridge) in a series of shifts, or " positions." If, for instance, the hand is shifted up about half an inch from its normal position (called the first, or natural position), the first finger, on the E string, will stop G, instead of F sharp, and the fourth finger will stop C, instead of B. If the hand is shifted about an inch farther up, the first finger will stop A, and the fourth finger D.

The skilled player will use ten, or even twelve, positions, but for the time being you need only concern yourself with five. Study the example below, which gives the first five positions of the A string, and then work out the five positions on the G, D, and E strings.

A String

The fingers of the left hand must be trained to fall firmly and smartly on exactly the right part of the strings; otherwise the notes will be out of tune. Hence the necessity for a discriminating ear. Scale practice and exercises will strengthen the fingers and make them supple.

Tone Production

The production of a clear singing tone is the most difficult part of violin playing, for tone is something *personal*, and there is no infallible method by which it may be acquired. The foundations are best laid by drawing long, straight bows. The bow should be held lightly, but sufficiently firmly to control it, and the tone produced with a light pressure of the wrist only, and not of the arm. The beginner should be content with quite a soft tone, provided it is evenly sustained. Scales should be practised for tone production by playing each note with a full bow, as slowly as possible.

Some Further Points of Technique

When two or more notes are to be played in the same stroke of the bow, a slur (see Chapter III, section 41) is placed over them. When two or more notes have both dots and a slur placed over them, they are to be played *staccato* in one stroke of the bow; that is, the bow is to be stopped between each note, instead of being drawn smoothly. All notes not included under a slur are to be played with separate bows.

If a string is touched very lightly at certain points, and not pressed down on to the fingerboard, it will produce high sounds of a light, flute-like quality. These sounds are called "natural harmonics," and are indicated by placing an O over the notes which are to be lightly touched. If a string is firmly stopped with the first finger and lightly touched with the fourth, an " artificial harmonic " will be produced, sounding two octaves higher than the stopped note. This is indicated by writing the note to be stopped as an ordinary note, and the note to be lightly touched as a diamond-shaped note a fourth higher.

Two notes on adjacent strings may be played at the same time to form a chord. The simplest chords are formed by playing on two adjacent open strings (G and D, D and A, or A and E).

Chords may also be formed by playing two stopped notes on adjacent strings, or one stopped note and one open string. Any two-note chord (even if both notes are open strings) is usually called a " double-stop." In playing double-stops it is necessary to attack them by means of a wrist action, in order that both notes may be sounded at precisely the same moment. Only a moderate amount of pressure should be applied, otherwise a harsh tone will result.

Three-note chords (triple-stops), and four-note chords (quadruple-stops) may also be played. In these chords only the two top notes can be sustained owing to the curvature of the bridge. In playing a three-note chord, attack the bottom and middle notes together, then attack and sustain the middle and top notes. In playing a four-note chord, first attack the two lowest notes, then attack and sustain the two highest notes.

When the word *pizzicato* (Italian for " plucked "), or its abbreviation *pizz*, appears in violin music, it means that the notes are to be plucked with the finger, instead of being played with the bow. The bow should be kept in the hand, and the string plucked with the fleshy part of the first finger, the thumb being kept against the finger-board. The resumption of bowing is indicated by the word *arco* (Italian for " bow ").

Sometimes a little three-pronged "mute," made of wood or metal, is placed on the bridge of the violin, and has the effect of attenuating the sound to a kind of silvery whisper. The use of the mute is indicated by the Italian words *con sordini;* the contradiction is *senza sordini.*

How to Study

When you have learnt how to hold the violin and bow, you should obtain a good method such as *The Violin:* Berthold Tours, ed. W. H. Reed (Novello), or *The Violin:* M. Crickboom (Schott). When you have made some progress with this, you can add *Twelve Preliminary Studies:* Herbert Kinsey (Associated Board), together with some easy solo pieces. Choose those that appeal to you most; nearly all publishers have a graded series of classical and light solos from which you can make your choice.

The repertory of the violin is a very large one, and includes a good deal of music written, or transcribed, by virtuoso violinists: Tartini, famous for his *Devil's Trill* Sonata, Sphor, De Beriot, Vieuxtemps, Wieniawski, and later Fritz Kreisler, whose admirable arrangements and compositions have become standard works.

If you have a violinist friend, there are a number of duets for two violins to choose from, including some easy ones by Richards, Chagrin, and Twinn (Novello). There are also some attractive suites for three violins, by Robert Donington and Charles Vale (Elkin).

If there is an amateur orchestra in your neighbourhood, join it as soon as you can. Orchestral playing is not only first-rate practice; it is also a hobby of which you will never grow tired.

E

THE VIOLA

This is a neglected instrument. Up to about the eighteenth century, it was simply used to double some other part in the orchestra. Even later, when the viola developed some sort of individuality of its own, the standard of playing was very low. Because it was seldom given any important music, it used to be considered easier to play than the violin, and for this reason it was often taken up by second-rate violinists, who were anxious to make quicker progress.

Later, under Lionel Tertis and other distinguished players, the viola acquired some of the dignity it deserved, but it has always suffered from the size of its repertory which, even to-day, is far too small.

The viola is tuned a perfect fifth below the violin, thus :

Music for the viola is written in the alto clef, with the occasional use of the treble clef for high passages. The tone has a veiled quality ; it is sometimes rather nasal, but on a full-size instrument (there are various sizes) it is rich and penetrating.

The technique of the viola is the same as that of the violin, except that there is a slightly larger stretch between the fingers on the finger-board, because of the lower pitch of the instrument. Apart from this, all the principles of violin technique which have already been discussed apply to the viola. Anyone who has studied the violin should be able to transfer to the viola quite easily.

The instrument should be carefully selected and

strung, as the viola is far more likely to have defects of tone than is the violin. It should be tested throughout its compass, as some violas have one or two "wolf" notes; a wolf note is heard as if two notes, perhaps a quarter of a tone apart, are sounding at the same time.

The two lowest strings (C and G) are both of gut covered with wire, and sometimes, after much use, this covering may work loose, causing the string to rattle when it is played on. It should then be replaced by a new string.

A special viola bow is used by most players, but some prefer a full-size violin bow of rather heavy design.

For the beginner, *Berthold Tour's Viola Method*, ed. and rev. Bernard Shore (Novello), may be recommended.

THE 'CELLO

The 'cello has much to commend it; it is a fine solo instrument and, next to the violin, the most useful member of the orchestra. Its repertory, though not so large as the violin's, is better than that of the viola. It is no more difficult to learn than the violin, and a player who has already mastered the violin will find that he can take up 'cello playing quite easily.

The 'cello is made in full, three-quarter, half, and quarter sizes. In appearance it is like a large violin or viola, except that it has a long metal "peg" which is used to support the instrument while it is being played, and which may be slid into the body of the instrument when not is use.

The 'cello is pitched an octave below the viola, and is tuned in perfect fifths, thus:

Although the 'cello is considerably larger than the violin the bow used is shorter (though heavier), so that in legato passages the 'cellist must change his bow more frequently than the violinist.

'Cello technique differs from that of the violin in many respects, although some principles are common to both instruments. The section on violin playing should be studied, therefore, so that you will be familiar with such terms as positions, double-stopping, *pizzicato*, and so on.

The 'cello is held by gripping it between the knees, the right knee being lowered so that it is out of the way of the bow. The metal " peg " should be so adjusted that the peg of the C string just clears the left hand lapel of the coat.

The direction of 'cello bowing is the reverse to that of violin bowing ; the violin bow points downwards towards the G string, whereas the 'cello bow points upwards towards the A string. The bow is held by placing the thumb (which should be slightly bent) in the angle made by the stick and the nut of the bow, so that the right side of the thumb touches the stick. The fingers should fall naturally around the stick, the little finger helping to balance it.

As in violin playing, the bow must be drawn parallel to the bridge, and it should be placed on the string about equidistant between the bridge and the end of the finger-board.

In the lower positions, the fingering of the 'cello differs from that of the violin, because of the greater distance between the notes on the finger-board. The 'cellist may stretch a semitone between any two adjacent fingers, and a tone between the first and second fingers, but not between the second and third, and the third and fourth fingers. The fingering is therefore less regular than that of the violin.

'Cello fingering may be best understood by studying the following chart of the scale of C major (one octave, ascending) starting on the open C string.

C	D	E	F	G	A	B	C
Open String	1	3	4	Open String	1	3	4

The hand is moved up the neck of the 'cello for the various positions, as on the violin. Above the fourth position, 'cello fingering is like that of the violin.

'Cello music is mostly written in the bass clef, but the tenor and treble clefs are used for high passages.

A good method for the beginner is *Foundations of 'Cello Playing* by Frederick Bye (Boosey & Hawkes).

THE DOUBLE-BASS

This is the largest instrument of the string group, and is only used in the orchestra, since it is too unwieldy for solo purposes.

The double-bass is similar in appearance to the 'cello except that is has sloping shoulders.

In the nineteenth century, three-stringed basses were in great favour, but the modern instrument usually has four strings tuned in fourths to the notes E, A, D, G. The music is normally written in the bass clef, and the tenor clef is occasionally used for high passages. But whichever clef is used, the music is always written an octave higher than it sounds.

The fingering of the bass, in the higher positions, is the same as that of the 'cello. In the lower positions, the maximum stretch between the first and fourth fingers is a tone, and between the first and second a semitone.

The double-bass player should be fairly tall (the instrument stands about six feet high), and he should

F

have strong fingers as the strings are thick and heavy to press down.

There is a good tutor by Adolph Lotter in the Langey Series (Boosey & Hawkes).

WIND INSTRUMENTS

The technique of the various wind instruments will only be described very briefly; to go into it fully, at least a chapter would be required for each instrument. But some general principles will be outlined, and methods mentioned from which fuller information can be obtained.

Wood-wind instruments are, broadly speaking, based upon the same principle as the old "penny whistle." You know the idea—six holes bored in a metal tube, and covered or uncovered by the fingers to produce different notes. If these holes are uncovered one by one, the notes of the major scale may be produced, and the intermediate semitones (or some of them, at least) may be obtained by "cross-fingering", that is, by covering a hole below the one which is sounding. Then, by using the same fingering and blowing harder into the whistle, the same series of notes may be produced an octave higher in pitch. Even so, there are several gaps in the scale, as well as many imperfect notes, because there are not enough fingers to control all the holes that ought to be bored in the whistle, to produce a perfect chromatic scale.

So numerous keys were fitted to wind instruments to facilitate the fingering, and about the middle of the nineteenth century a system was devised by a Munich flute-player, Theobald Boehm, whereby holes could be cut in the proper positions, and yet be easily opened and closed by the fingers. The essence of the " Boehm system", as it is now called, is that four holes come under the control of three fingers.

All modern flutes and oboes are designed on the Boehm system, and when purchasing an instrument it is important to bear this in mind. Most, but not all, modern clarinet players use Boehm system instruments.

Brass instruments are based on quite a different principle. Many people are puzzled how a trumpet, or a French horn, can play a chromatic scale with only three keys (more properly called " valves " or " pistons "). The explanation, quite simply, is this. When a sound is produced by agitating air in a tube, it is rarely heard alone ; there are sounding with it various parts of what is called the " harmonic series," which is the only *natural* scale in existence, and which ascends by irregular intervals; an octave, a fifth, a fourth, thirds, tones, and semitones. Any one sound in the series may be made prominent to the apparent isolation of the others. Different brass instruments use different sections of the harmonic series, according to the length of their tubes. The individual harmonics are brought into prominence by the lip action of the player.

The gaps between the harmonics are filled in by the use of valves, or pistons (French horn, trumpet, cornet, and tuba), or by the manipulation of a slide (trombone). The effect of either device is the same ; the tube is lengthened, and the pitch is consequently lowered.

The trumpet, cornet and French horn are provided with three pistons. When each piston is pressed down with the finger, an additional little piece of tubing is added to the main tube, and when the piston is released, the extra tubing is cut off again. One of the pistons lowers the pitch of the entire harmonic series by a semi-tone, another by a tone, and a third by a tone and a half. Two, or three, pistons may be used in combination ; if, for instance, the tone and the tone-and-a-half pistons are used together, the pitch will be lowered two-and-a-half tones, and if all three pistons are used, the pitch will be lowered three tones.

The trombone has a sliding tube which may be placed in seven different positions. This provides for the lowering of the harmonic series in six stages of a semitone each ; the second position is a semitone below the first, or fundamental, position, the third position is a semitone below the second, and so on.

THE FLUTE

The modern flute has a compass of three octaves.

The instrument, as we know it to-day, is made up of three pieces :

(1) The Head, which is more or less conical, and is plugged at one end with a cork or " stopper," and in which is cut the mouth-hole, or " embouchure." The embouchure is partly covered by the lower lip of the player, who directs his breath *across* it, so that it strikes the opposite edge.

(2) The Body, a cylindrical tube which carries the system of keys which are manipulated by the fingers of the player.

(3) The Foot-joint, which is added to allow the two bottom semitones, C and C sharp, to be produced.

The fingering for each octave is much the same, and the upper octaves are produced by " over-blowing," that is, by increasing the wind-pressure, which brings the "harmonics" into action, instead of the fundamental sound.

The modern flute is made either of wood or of metal, of which silver is the favourite. The tone-colour varies considerably at different parts of the compass. The lowest octave has a thick, velvety tone, which is rather easily covered up by other instruments. The middle octave is smooth and limpid, somewhat resembling the voice of a boy singer. The top octave is brilliant and penetrating, the two highest semitones being very difficult to play softly.

Rapid passages and trills are easy and effective. When nimble passages are played, double- or triple-tonguing is often used. In this kind of tonguing the player articulates T-K, and T-K-T, and is thus able to play a succession of staccato notes with the utmost rapidity.

The flute repertory contains sonatas and solo pieces by Bach, Handel, Haydn, Mozart and Schubert, and by a number of modern composers, as well as some chamber music for flute with other instruments. As a solo instrument the flute is charming, and well suited to an average-sized room. In the orchestra it is frequently given important solo passages.

The *Flute Tutor* by Langey (Boosey & Hawkes) is excellent for the beginner.

The concert piccolo, or octave flute, is pitched an octave above the concert flute, and its music sounds an octave higher than the written notes. The written compass is the same as that of the flute, except that the two lowest semitones are not available. The lower notes of the piccolo are weak, but the higher notes are shrill and penetrating. The second (or third) flute-player in an orchestra often plays either flute or piccolo, as the technique of both is similar.

THE OBOE

The oboe consists of a conical tube, expanding at the lower end into a bell. The tube is usually made in three sections, the uper and lower joints, and the bell. The double reed, from which t   soun   duced, consists of two thin str   astened   small metal tube or "staple," so   a tiny space is l   tween them.

The normal co   ass is:

Some players can reach notes a few semitones higher.

The tone, in the hands of a good player, is penetrating but sweet, and is equally charming in *legato* and *staccato* playing. Tone production is more difficult than on the flute or clarinet. The reed is placed between the lips, which cover the teeth and form a sort of cushion, and the beginning of every phrase is "attacked" by placing the tongue against the reed, and then withdrawing it to allow the breath to pass. This is called "single-tongueing." the only kind of tonguing which can be used on the oboe, because of the position of the reed in the mouth.

The management of the breath usually presents some difficulty. The player must take in just sufficient breath to play each phrase, and often a quick half-breath must be taken in the middle of a phrase

The reed of an oboe is very delicate and great care must be taken not to damage it, as a fine tone can only be obtained when the reed is in perfect condition. Many players make their own reeds (an operation requiring some skill, and a few special tools), as ready-made reeds are not always to be relied upon.

The cor anglais (or English horn) is pitched a perfect fifth below the oboe. In the orchestra it is usually played by one of the oboe players, and for this reason its music is always written a perfect fifth higher than it sounds, so that it may be read without difficulty. The written compass is the same as that of the oboe, except that the lowest semitone (B flat) is missing.

The cor anglais, in appearance, is longer than the oboe, and terminates in a globular bell. The reed is placed in a metal crook which is bent back to meet the player's lips.

The tone is smooth and rich, and peculiarly adapted to melancholy music. The fingering and technique are the same as those of the oboe.

The oboe repertory is small, but contains some attractive works. One of the best methods for the beginner is that by Langey (Boosey & Hawkes).

THE CLARINET

The clarinet is descended from a mediaeval instrument called the "Chalumeau", but the modern type of clarinet did not come into regular use until about Mozart's time.

It is a single reed instrument consisting of a mouthpiece, a cylindrical tube, and a bell. The tube, not being conical like that of the flute and oboe, overblows a twelfth instead of an octave.

Because of this, there is a gap between the octave and the twelfth which is filled in by a system of fingering which is not entirely satisfactory. This part of the compass, therefore, is rather dull and lifeless. The lower notes of the clarinet have a rich, oily quality. The upper part of the compass is best; it is clear, even, and expressive. The clarinet has great agility (it replaces the violin in the military band) and greater powers of playing *pianissimo*, and of swelling or diminishing the tone, than any other wind instrument.

The orchestral clarinet player uses two instruments, one pitched in B flat and the other in A. The written compass of both is the same:

Music for the B flat clarinet sounds a tone lower than written; music for the A clarinet sounds a minor third lower than written. Thus, if the note C is written, it sounds B flat on the B flat clarinet, and A on the A clarinet. The fingering and technique of both instruments is the same, so that the player can change from one instrument to another without difficulty. If only one instrument is purchased, choose the B flat clarinet; it is the more useful of the two.

The bass clarinet in B flat is pitched an octave below the ordinary B flat instrument, and the written compass is the same. Because of the great length of the tube, the lower end is curved upwards in the shape of a bell, and the upper end curved inwards to bring the mouthpiece nearer to the player's mouth.

The clarinet reed is a flat piece of cane, held to the mouthpiece by a metal clamp.

Before purchasing a clarinet tutor, make sure that the system is the right one. There is a good tutor on the Boehm system by Frank and Thurston (Boosey & Hawkes).

THE BASSOON

This is a double-reed instrument of the oboe family. The compass is:

The music is written in the bass and tenor clefs. The tube is so long that it is made in two sections which are united at the lower end. The reed is fixed to a curved metal tube. The tone is powerful and reedy.

The bassoon's natural function is to provide the bass of the wood-wind group. It is also used as a solo instrument, and as such it is capable of producing comic effects. That is why it used to be called "the clown of the orchestra".

The double-bassoon is a large and ponderous instrument with a heavy and obtrusive tone. Its music is written an octave higher than it sounds.

Langey's *Bassoon Tutor* (Boosey & Hawkes) may be recommended.

BRASS INSTRUMENTS

The French horn in F is a coiled tube, narrow at one end and expanding into a large bell at the other. A funnel-shaped mouthpiece is inserted into the narrow end. The double-horn, often used by professional players, has two sets of tubing operated from the same three valves; a fourth valve enables the player to switch from F to B flat, and vice versa.

Horn music is written in the treble (or sometimes bass) clef, a perfect fifth above the real sounds. The written compass of the horn in F is:

Sometimes, in order to get a certain quality of tone, the hand is inserted into the bell, and the notes so produced are said to be "stopped." A mute placed in the bell gives a somewhat similar effect.

The normal tone may be mellow or brassy, according to the action of the player's lips. Tone production requires great skill as the player must "feel" the notes before he can produce them, and until he can do this instinctively he will often find himself "wobbling" off the note.

Before the application of valves to horns and trumpets, it was only possible to play the notes of the harmonic series, so that the player had a very limited number of notes at his disposal. To overcome this difficulty the natural horns and trumpets were provided with a number of crooks—pieces of tubing of various sizes which could be changed according to the key of the music. To allow the player to change from one crook to another without difficulty, the composer "transposed" his horn and trumpet parts, so that they sounded higher or lower than the actual written notes. The composer of to-day invariably writes for the horn in F, and the modern player usually prefers to keep to this one crook. This means that when playing the music of the older composers, in which the horns are crooked in other keys, the player himself must make the necessary transposition. If, for example, a horn part written for the E flat crook is played on the F crook, the player must read the part a tone lower than he would if he were using the E flat crook. Similarly a B flat trumpet player, reading music written for a trumpet crooked in another key, must make a mental transposition.

The modern trumpet is pitched in B flat or C; the B flat instrument may be put into A (but seldom is), either by pulling out a sliding tube, or by turning a tap which automatically includes or shuts off an additional piece of tubing. The written range is:

This sounds (*a*) on the C trumpet as written; (*b*) on the B flat trumpet a tone lower; (*c*) on the A trumpet a minor third lower.

The cornet in B flat has the same compass as the B flat trumpet and is similar in appearance, but shorter and tubbier. It is more used in military and brass bands than in the orchestra.

Both the trumpet and cornet use a cup-shaped mouthpiece, but the cornet mouthpiece is deeper than that of the trumpet. Cornet technique is much easier to acquire than trumpet technique, because the cornet "speaks" more easily, and the notes can be produced with greater certainty. Cornet tone is more mellow and less brassy than trumpet tone. Double- and triple-tonguing is possible on both instruments.

Three kinds of trombone are used in the orchestra. The tenor trombone in B flat is written in the tenor and bass clefs, and the bass trombone in G in the bass clef. The compass is:

There is also a tenor-bass trombone having the combined compass of the two instruments.

Owing to the slide action, a true legato is not possible. The mouthpiece is usually cup-shaped, and is held to the player's lips by the left hand, which also supports the instrument. The slide is controlled by the right hand, either by a wrist or an arm movement. The bass trombone slide is so long that a jointed handle is fitted to allow it to be fully extended.

The tuba in F is a heavy brass instrument with four valves, similar in appearance to the big brass basses which are often seen in military bands.

There is an excellent series of tutors for brass instruments by Langey (Boosey & Hawkes), which includes the French horn, trumpet, cornet, tenor trombone and saxophone.

WHY NOT THE HARP?

The harp, perhaps the most beautiful of all instruments, is now sadly neglected. In Victorian days, a harp was often found in the drawing-room of a mansion (though it was not always played upon), but nowadays very few amateurs take it up. This is to be regretted, for the harp should be heard more often. It is equally effective as a solo instrument, as an accompaniment to vocal or instrumental music, or in the orchestra.

Unfortunately, lessons from an experienced harpist are essential if real progress is to be made, and good teachers are not often to be found. The beginner would find a knowledge of the piano, and of the rules of harmony, valuable assets.

The compass of
the modern harp is:

Music for the harp is written on two staves, exactly like piano music.

THE RECORDER

The recorder is a wooden (or plastic) flute of the end-blown type (unlike the modern flute which is side-blown). After centuries of use it fell into decline, and was revived largely through the efforts of Arnold Dolmetsch. Its appeal is both to children and adults; it is inexpensive, and not difficult to learn.

The recorder has six holes for the three middle fingers of each hand, plus one for the left hand little finger, and one for the right hand thumb. There are normally five sizes, of which the descant is the most usual (range two octaves, starting from C above middle C). Experienced players often prefer the tone of the treble (a fifth below the descant), or the tenor (an octave below the descant). There is also a sopranino (a fourth above the descant) and a bass (a fifth below the tenor).

The gentle tone of the recorder is well suited to the delightful music, both period and modern, for solo recorder and for two or more recorders, with or without piano accompaniment. Imogen Holst's *The Book of the Descant Recorder* (Boosey & Hawkes) may be recommended.

THE GUITAR

The appearance of the modern Spanish guitar is too well known to need description. The six strings, which are tuned in fourths and thirds, are plucked with the fingers, or (for popular music) with a small plectrum. Guitar music, which is written in the treble clef, an octave higher than the actual sounds, often contains chords of from two to six notes.

Because of its weak tone, the guitar is sometimes amplified; in addition to the standard electric model with six strings, there is also a four-string bass guitar. The cost may be from £15 (non-electric) to £400 (electric).

CHAPTER VIII

THE ORGAN FAMILY

The Pipe Organ

Pipe organs vary considerably in size and detail, so that any description must necessarily apply to one particular instrument. The organ, an average Three Manual organ of moderate size, will be described from the point of view of the player as he sits on the organ stool.

In front of him the three manuals (or keyboards) rise one above the other. The middle, the most important, manual is called the Great Organ. The highest manual is called the Swell Organ, and the pipes belonging to it are enclosed in a box with movable shutters. By means of a pedal controlled by the player's feet (called the Swell Pedal), these shutters may be gradually opened or closed, so producing an increase or diminution in the volume of sound. The lowest manual is called the Choir Organ.

On each side of the manuals are rows of "stop" controls; either handles, which may be pulled out or pushed in, or "tablets" or "keys". Each stop-handle, or other device, controls a "stop", that is, a row of pipes of different pitch all producing the same tone-colour, and each bears the name of the stop it controls and also a numeral which indicates the length, in feet, of the longest pipe belonging to that stop. The pipes of a stop marked eight feet will sound at the same pitch as the corresponding notes on the piano, those of a stop marked four feet, or two feet, one or two octaves higher, and those of a stop marked sixteen feet an octave below normal pitch.

Each manual has its own set of pipes, and is therefore independent of the other manuals.

Beneath the player's feet is a wooden keyboard called the Pedal Organ, which also has its own set of stops.

Above the pedal-board is a row of special pedals called "combination pedals". By pressing these, certain fixed combinations of stops may be brought into use without raising the hands from the keys. The same result may be brought about by pressing a series of pistons which are placed in rows between the manuals.

Several of the stop-handles are marked "coupler", and may be used to connect two of the manuals, so that by pressing down a key on one manual the corresponding key on the other manual is depressed. The pedal organ may also be coupled to any of the manuals, and there is another coupler which causes notes an octave above to sound with the notes played.

The selection of the most suitable stops is called "registering".

The compass of the organ manuals is five octaves, starting from the C on the second leger line below the bass stave; and of the pedal organ two-and-a-half octaves, starting from the same note.

The average three manual organ will contain about thirty-six stops and couplers, allocated as follows:

> Swell organ: ten stops
> Great organ: ten stops
> Choir organ: five stops
> Pedal organ: five stops
> Couplers: six stops

The stop-handles for the swell organ, the couplers, and the pedal organ will be on the player's left, and those for the great and choir organs on the player's right.

The tone of certain stops may be given a throbbing quality by the use of a device called the "tremulant", which is set in motion by the hand or the foot, and which should be used with discretion.

The organ stops are divided into several groups which may be classified as follows :

DIAPASON STOPS

The foundation tone of the organ. The most usual stops are Open Diapason (8 feet), Stopped Diapason (8 feet), Double Diapason (16 feet), Principal (4 feet), Fifteenth (2 feet), Bourdon (16 feet, pedal stop), Voix Céleste (8 feet), Dulciana (8 feet), Sub-Bourdon (16 feet), and Gerdact (8 feet).

STRING STOPS

Resembling the tone of string instruments. The most usual are Gamba (8 feet), Violone (8 feet), Violoncello (8 feet, pedal stop), Echo Gamba (8 feet), Geigen (8 feet).

REED STOPS

Resembling the tone of the orchestral instruments after which they are named. The most usual are Clarinet (8 feet), Oboe (8 feet), Trumpet (8 feet), Cornopean, or Horn (8 feet), Vox Humana (8 feet), and Trombone (16 feet, pedal stop).

FLUTE STOPS

Resembling the tone of a flute. The most usual are Suabe Flute (4 feet), Harmonic Flute (4 feet), Piccolo (2 feet), Claribel (8 feet), and Bass Flute (8 feet, pedal stop).

MIXTURE STOP

A stop that has two, three, or four pipes to each manual key.

TWELFTH STOP

A stop of $2\frac{3}{4}$ feet sounding a twelfth above the notes played.

The 8 feet stops are the most useful on each of the manuals. The Mixture and Twelfth Stops are always used in conjunction with 8, 4, or 2 feet stops, to which they add new tone-colour. The "Voix Céleste" has two pipes to each note, one tuned a little sharper than the other. It is always used with some other stop, such as the "Echo Gamba", to which it adds a wavy, mysterious quality. The "Vox Humana" is supposed to imitate the human voice, although the imitation is not particularly accurate. It is usually drawn in conjunction with the "Tremolo" stop.

The fundamental difference between organ and piano technique has already been discussed in Chapter II.

The organist may play with both hands on the same manual, or with each hand on a different manual. The art of organ registration is acquired by experience, and by carefully listening to the effect of different combinations of stops. No description of the tone-quality of the stops can take the place of an aural demonstration. A balance must be achieved between the pedal organ and the manuals by drawing appropriate stops on each.

The 8 feet tone should be the basis of organ tone-colour, and should be used for accompanying a solo stop. The pedals should be coupled to the manuals on which the accompaniment is being played.

The effect of a *crescendo*, or more accurately of the building up of tone, may be produced by gradually adding suitable stops to a soft 8 feet foundation tone. The opposite effect may be produced by taking away the stops one by one.

Single stops, or stops of one family (Diapason, Flute, String or Reed) should mostly be used, as the frequent mixing of different stops soon becomes irritating. On small organs with few stops, variety of tone-colour may be obtained by playing from time to time on 16 or 4 feet stops.

The pedal organ has long and short keys, which may be compared to the black and white manual keys. The keys are played with the toe or heel, and are pressed down, not struck, by the movement of the ankle. In scale passages, one foot is often passed behind the other.

Organ music is written on three staves, the top and middle staves (treble and bass clefs) for the manuals, and the bottom stave (bass clef) for the pedals.

The repertory of the organ is limited compared to that of the piano. Outstanding are the organ works of Bach and Handel; the sonatas of Rheinberger and Max Reger are also noteworthy.

The beginner should get *The Oxford Organ Method* by C. H. Trevor (Oxford University Press). This contains 18 complete short pieces, as well as numerous exercises carefully selected from major organ works.

The Harmonium

The Harmonium was first introduced in 1840, and the name was originated by Alexandre Debain, who, if he did not actually invent the instrument, at any rate improved it considerably.

The sound is produced by the pressure of air on thin metal tongues known as "free reeds", because they do not completely close the aperture in which they vibrate.

The compass is the same as the manual compass of the organ (five octaves), and the music is written on two staves like piano music.

The harmonium usually has a row of ten stop-handles, of which eight bear a number, and two are left blank. Each of the numbered handles acts on a different set of reeds. Those on the left of the keyboard, numbered 4, 3, 2, 1, control the bass stops, and affect only the lower half of the instrument up to, and including, E on the first line of the treble stave. The stop-handles on the right of the keyboard, numbered 1, 2, 3, 4, control the treble stops, and affect only the upper half of the instrument, starting from F on the first space of the stave.

The usual stops are as follows :

Bass		*Treble*	
1.—Cor Anglais	8 feet pitch	Flute	8 feet pitch
2.—Bourdon	16 feet pitch	Clarinette	16 feet pitch
3.—Clarion	4 feet pitch	Fifre	4 feet pitch
4.—Bassoon	8 feet pitch	Hautbois	8 feet pitch

The two blank stop-handles are usually placed in the centre. The one on the right is the " Grand Jeu " : the one on the left the " Expression Stop."

The Grand Jeu brings all the stops into action at once, so that the full power of the instrument is heard. To understand the use of the Expression Stop it is first necessary to describe the manner of blowing.

Two treadles are provided for the feet, which are moved alternately, one rising while the other is being depressed. The treadles feed the bellows, and the wind created is stored in a reservoir which must be kept regularly supplied with air. When the Expression Stop is used, this reservoir is cut off, allowing the air to act directly on the reeds. Thus the tone may be increased or decreased by blowing more or less strongly, and many fine shades of expression obtained.

In addition to the stops there are two octave-couplers similar to those on the organ. The Treble Coupler (also called the Octave) causes notes an octave above to sound with the notes played. The Bass Coupler, or Octave, does the same with notes an octave below those played. There is also a Tremolo device which, like the tremolo stop on the organ, should be used with great care.

Below the keyboard are two wooden flaps called "Kneel Swells", which are pressed outwards by the knees. The one on the right produces a *crescendo* or *diminuendo;* the one on the left gradually brings all the stops into play, cancelling them as it is released. By using both knee swells, the loudest tone possible may be produced.

The treadles must be worked evenly by the feet and sufficient air, but no more, provided. When all the stop-handles are drawn, the treadling will have to be more rapid than when only one or two soft stops are used. Skilful blowing is especially necessary when the expression stop is used.

The American Organ

The technique is similar to that of the harmonium, with one or two exceptions. The smaller instruments have only six stops, the stop-handles bearing names and figures showing the length of the stops in feet. There is no expression stop.

Some of the largest American organs have two or more manuals and a pedal-board, the technique being similar to that of the pipe organ.

The Electronic Organ

The popularity of the electronic organ has increased enormously in recent years. Although the tone quality is bound to differ from that of a pipe organ, which is still preferred for serious music in concert halls and churches, the electronic organ has the considerable advantage of taking up relatively little space.

The range of electronic organs starts with one-manual models with self-contained amplifier and speakers, and ends with cathedral models with two manuals, pedal board and separate reverberation systems designed to reproduce the acoustics of a large concert hall. Some of the smaller organs have a "harmonising" device which makes it possible to play chords with one finger.

There are several types of electronic organ. In the Hammond organ the fundamental tones are produced by tone wheels which rotate close to an electromagnet. Other types of organ use systems of electrostatic generators, either rotating (Compton organ) or vibrating (Wurlitzer organ); in the latter type reeds are made to vibrate by means of a fan, so that the system is not wholly electronic.

In another type of organ the tones are generated by valves or transistors; transistorised organs (such as the Fairfisa-Ballata) have the advantage of remaining in tune if there is a voltage drop in the mains supply.

Useful instruction books, both by Arthur Wildman (Bosworth), are *The Belwin Hammond Organ Course* and *From Piano to Hammond Organ,* a transition course for the pianist.

CHAPTER IX

PRACTICAL SINGING

Your Voice and how to use it

You may have read the verse about the centipede. He was perfectly happy until one day the toad, in fun, asked him " When you run, which leg comes after which ? " This so upset the poor centipede that he lay helpless in a ditch, trying to find the answer.

Some singers are like that. They read books on the anatomy of the vocal organs ; they discover that they have a larynx, an epiglottis, a diaphragm, and a pair of vocal cords. They are shown pictures of the ribs, and the lungs, and the Crico-Arytenoid muscles. The only thing they are not taught, in fact, is to sing. They are so busy with physiology that they have no time to listen to the sounds which they are producing.

Singing is, or should be, a natural process. Some of us are born with voices which, in the course of years, develop into instruments of beauty and power, without any ordered training or study. Others have vocal gifts which may lie latent until they are shown how to use them. But whether the voice is natural or cultivated the great thing is that it shall *appear* to be natural. Many an untrained and imperfect voice has greater appeal than the most efficiently trained one, because we feel the first voice to be sincere, and the second artificial.

For centuries voice training has abounded in weird and wonderful theories, in methods that have been exalted by some and decried by others. Many useful discoveries have been made, but one fact has too often been overlooked ; the key to voice training lies in the mind of the singer. For the greatest attribute of the singer is the ability to pass judgment on his own voice.

We all know people with ugly speaking voices, voices so harsh and discordant that they jangle in our ears like cracked bells. And we know other voices which are soft and mellow ; that soothe us and play upon our emotions. The difference lies not in the fact that one set of vocal organs is superior to the other, or that one speaker's voice has been trained and perfected, while the other speaker has received no training ; it is simply that the ugly speaker does not know how to listen to his own voice.

The first thing you must learn, then, is to judge your own voice. Once you have mastered the art of critical listening, you will be well on the way to perfecting your voice.

Developing your Voice

Voices which are naturally perfect and require no training are comparatively rare. The technical equipment of a singer may be considered under two main headings ; the ability to produce a full and beautiful tone, and the ability to pronounce words distinctly and correctly. We shall consider tone production first of all.

The voice is the only natural musical instrument in existence, but it is built upon similar principles as that part of an organ known as a reed-pipe. Both voice and reed-pipe have an apparatus for wind-supply ; the lungs supply the voice, and the wind chest supplies the reed-pipe. The reed-pipe has a strip of metal called a " reed," which produces sound when it is made to vibrate ; the voice has two tiny elastic strips of cartilage, each about half an inch long, known as " vocal cords," which act as sound-producing reeds when breath is passed between them. The sound produced by the reed of the reed-pipe, or by the vocal cords of the voice, may amount to little more than a feeble squeak; the pipe itself, and the mouth and nasal cavities, act as resonators, developing the squeak into a full and vibrant tone.

The vocal cords act automatically, and no conscious effort is needed to adjust them. The singer has only to imagine a particular note, and the vocal cords, by a process which nobody has yet been able to explain, immediately assume the correct tension. It is easy, of course, to imagine a wrong note, or one which is out of tune, especially if sufficient attention has not been paid to training the ear. But apart from this consideration, the singer need not worry about the action of the vocal cords, so long as he realizes that they must be allowed to vibrate freely and easily, and that they must not be strained by forcing the voice.

The breathing and resonating apparatuses do not, unfortunately, function entirely automatically, and the singer must give thought to them if he is to produce the right quality of tone.

It has been said that the mouth and nasal cavities act as resonators to the voice. It follows, then, that the quality of tone is conditioned by the shape of the mouth, and that the shape of the mouth depends upon the position of the lips, the tongue, the soft palate (the soft, fleshy substance which forms the back part of the roof of the mouth), and the lower jaw.

These movable parts of the mouth and throat assume different positions when different vowels are sung. Sing " ah " in front of a mirror, softly and with the mouth fairly wide open, and watch the position of the tongue and soft palate. The tongue will lie flat, the soft palate will be raised, and the tone will be round and full. Now try to sing " ee," keeping the mouth and the throat in exactly the same position. You will find it practically impossible to prevent the lips from coming closer together.

When you sing " ee," the tone will probably be thin and reedy, and not at all like the full, round tone of " ah." But suppose you are singing a word which contains both these vowels. It clearly will not do if the " ee " is thin, and the " ah " is fat. Your problem, then, is to equalize the tone of the vowels, so that each is satisfying, and all are well balanced.

How may this equality of tone be obtained ? First of all, it must be repeated that the ear is the ultimate judge of tone, for the simple reason that you cannot, except when you are practising in front of a mirror, see what your throat is doing while you are singing. But different kinds of tone produce different physical sensations, and if these sensations are memorized they will assist the ear in the selection of good tone.

The reason why the " ee " tone sounded thin and reedy was probably because part of the breath was allowed to escape through the vocal cords, without being converted into tone. The cure for this is a simple one. Close the lips, place the tip of the tongue against the roof of the mouth, and hum softly on a medium note (say G above middle C). Do this once or twice until you are able to produce a rich, resonant tone, and make a careful mental note of the sensation produced (a sort of buzzing around the nose and upper teeth). Then, keeping the sensation in mind, change the hum to " ee." You will find that the " ee " will now be rich and full.

We have seen that various parts of the mouth and throat act as resonators, and the sensation of so directing the vocalized breath that it strikes against a particular resonator is called " placing " the voice. Thus, the voice may be directed forward, or backward, or to the middle.

If " ah " is sung, followed by " oo," the sensation experienced will be of the tone leaping forward from the back of the throat to the lips.

Forward tone, such as that produced when placing an " m " or an " n " before a vowel, is the most useful tone for the beginner to practise, because the untrained voice has a natural tendency to become throaty. You are recommended to practise the humming exercise with each vowel in turn, until you are able to sing the vowels in succession with exact equality of tone. When, but only when, forward production has been mastered, you will find that you can add richness and colour to the voice by placing it a little farther back, midway between the soft palate and the teeth.

If you sing a scale on, say, " ay," you will probably find that one or two notes are unequal in tone, and are liable to crack or break. The best way to overcome this inequality is to practise the scale with soft, round tone, concentrating on keeping the throat absolutely free. You will soon feel if it is tightening up.

The range of the voice may be extended upwards or downwards by the practice of scales and special exercises, but do not be in too much of a hurry to increase it. For the first few months you should be content with a range of about an octave and a half (you may even start with an octave, or less), and as you make progress, you can add a note or two at a time, at each end of the voice. If you are a soprano, for instance, you might start practising from about D (the note above middle C), up to about G (an octave and three notes above D). This is only a generalization, for the development of the voice is such an individual matter that few definite rules can be given. The deciding factor must always be whether or not the notes can be produced naturally, and without effort.

Classification of Voices

No two singers have vocal organs which are exactly alike, and no two voices have exactly the same range and sonority of tone. But a general classification of voices has come into existence in which there are four main divisions : Soprano, Contralto, Tenor, and Bass. These are subdivided into Mezzo-Soprano, and Baritone. In classifying voices, both the compass and the vocal quality has to be considered.

Female voices are classified as :

Soprano

This is the highest voice of all and is divided into three classes :

(1) Dramatic Soprano, a powerful voice, especially suited to the performance of " declamatory " music, that is, music which depicts anger, excitement, rapture, or other strong emotions.

(2) Lyric Soprano, a lighter voice which is more agile than the dramatic soprano. This is the most usual form of soprano voice.

(3) Coloratura Soprano, a voice with a bright, penetrating, flute-like quality, a high range, and an ability to sing quick passages with great agility, and to perform many kinds of vocal acrobatics.

The compass of the average soprano voice is from middle C to the C two octaves above, but in exceptional voices this compass may be extended by several notes, either upwards or downwards.

Mezzo-Soprano

This voice combines the brightness of the soprano with the richness of the contralto, and has a full, mellow tone, which is also very flexible. The average compass is from the B flat below middle C upwards for about two octaves. The mezzo-soprano is the commonest of female voices.

Contralto

The true contralto voice is rare; it has a rich, heavy quality, and though it is less flexible than the higher voices, it is capable of greater expression. The compass is usually slightly less than two octaves, starting from the G below middle C.

Male voices are classified as:

Tenor

The highest male voice, which is divided into two classes:

(1) Light or Lyric Tenor, a brilliant, flexible voice, the male counterpart of the lyric soprano.

(2) Heavy or Robust Tenor, a full, vigorous voice, corresponding to the dramatic soprano.

The average tenor voice has a compass of about an octave and a half, starting from the E below middle C. The lower notes are usually poor and weak, compared with those of a baritone.

Baritone

The commonest variety of male voice, midway between the tenor and the bass. It is more flexible than the bass, and deeper than the tenor. There are Light and Heavy Baritones, the light voice using more of a tenor quality than the heavy one.

Bass

The bass is the deepest male voice, and is divided into two classes:

(1) Basso Cantante or Lyric Bass, sometimes called

Bass-Baritone; it has qualities similar to those of the other lyric voices.

(2) Basso Profundo, or Deep Bass, the most powerful voice with the lowest range.

The average compass starts two or three notes below that of the baritone, and extends for about an octave and a half.

During childhood, boys and girls have much the same voices. At puberty the boy's vocal chords rapidly lengthen, and after a period during which the voice is said to be " breaking " it settles an octave or so lower than before. The girl's voice also alters a good deal, but the change is more gradual and less noticeable. It is now generally accepted that boys and girls who have been singing from an early age may continue to do so, in a quiet way, during adolescence; but it is usually inadvisable to begin serious training before the age of seventeen or eighteen.

It has been said that the classification of voices is conditioned not only by the compass but also by the quality. This means that although a singer may have the compass of a tenor voice, he cannot be considered a tenor if his voice is not of tenor quality. It is not unknown for the quality of the voice to change completely during its development, and because of this several well-known singers have started their professional careers as tenors and then changed to baritones, and vice versa.

Music for female voices is always written in the treble clef, but either the treble or the bass clef may be used for male voices. The tenor, baritone, or bass should, therefore, have a knowledge of both clefs. When the treble clef is used, the notes are always written an octave higher than they actually sound, which makes them easier to read.

How to Sing Words

Song is really a combination of two arts, music and poetry. Ideally, each should be the complement of the other, but however skilfully the composer may blend them together, the ultimate responsibility for keeping them in this state of wedded bliss falls on the performer. He, too often, neglects to fulfil his trust, with the result that the words are sacrificed to the music, and the song loses its meaning.

It should be realised that most Englishmen speak very badly. This is largely due to laziness, since good speech demands some conscious effort, and considerable movement of the lips and mouth. If we are not prepared to make this effort our speech becomes dull, almost without inflexion, and often very indistinct. When we want to say " thank you " we make a sound like " queue," and when we want to say " goodbye " we make do with " bye." Is it any wonder, then, that when we try to sing nobody can understand what we are saying ?

In singing, the vowel sounds are often sustained considerably longer than in speech, and the first thing to be learnt, therefore, is to pronounce them correctly. The pure sounds of the vowels should never be sacrificed on the grounds of expediency ; how often do we hear a singer pronounce " love " as " lawve," simply to facilitate tone production.

Some of the vowel sounds require special attention. OO as in *two*, AH as in *jar*, A as in *play*, and E as in *me*, should be practised until the pronunciation is perfect. OO and O should be formed with the lips only, and the back of the throat should not be expanded.

The diphthongs, in which two vowel sounds are made into one, also need care. OI as in *joy*, for instance, is formed from AW and I (as in *it*). I as in *lie*, is formed from AH and I (as in *it*). When these diphthongs are sung, the first vowel sound must be sustained, and the second made as short as possible. In this way the common error of pronouncing light as *lah-eet*, and joy as *joy-ee*, may be avoided.

The general indistinctness of speech in song is frequently caused by failure to articulate the consonants distinctly. " Light and love " is often pronounced " ligh tan love." In correcting these errors, care must be taken not to go to the other extreme and sing " Lighter ander lover." A compromise may be effected by pronouncing the final consonant of each word in a whisper, so that it is audible without being obtrusive.

Consonants such as P and B, and D and J, are often confused ; thus we get " bowerful " for " powerful," and " dew " for " jew." It is important to know how these consonants should be produced. P and B are both formed by starting with closed lips ; P is more explosive than B, and needs to be articulated more crisply. T and D are formed with the tip of the tongue. J and Z are articulated with the middle of the tongue. R should be trilled (rolled) by the tongue, except when it comes at the end of a word. Consonants such as B, G, and D are often wrongly preceded by a kind of buzzing sound : Urbee, Urgee, Urdee. S and X require special care to avoid hissing them.

Some useful exercises for the practice of consonants and vowels will be found at the end of the chapter.

The Art of Breathing

The voice, being a wind instrument, must be properly supplied with breath.

The first thing you must learn about breathing is that many people control the breath naturally well, and that they should not concern themselves with methods of breathing, or try to practise elaborate exercises. If you have learned to walk, you will not gain much by studying the anatomy of the human leg. And if you do not walk as easily or as gracefully as you would wish to, a little thought and a simple exercise or two will do you more good than all the books on anatomy in the world. If you find difficulty in breathing easily and naturally, you will quickly discover this when you start to sing.

Breathing consists of two acts ; breathing in and breathing out. In singing, sounds have often to be sustained longer than in speech, so that it is necessary to breathe more deeply. The difficulty of breathing is not so much in taking in a sufficient quantity of breath, as in knowing how to use it after it has been taken in. The breath is the motive power of the voice, and the singer has to learn not to waste it, but to transform it all into sound.

The process of correct breathing will best be understood if it is described in the simplest possible terms. When you breathe in, do so silently, slowly, and deeply, as if you were inhaling the fragrance of a beautiful rose. As you breathe, imagine that you are about to yawn, and your throat will assume the correct position (called an " open " throat). When you breathe out, imagine that you are sighing deeply.

Remember that deep breathing is just an extension of ordinary breathing, and that it must be effortless, with not the slightest feeling of tension or rigidity. In singing, breath must be taken in through the mouth as well as the nose, for there is no other way of taking breath so quickly and silently. The shoulders should never be raised while the breath is being inhaled.

Never think about your breathing when you are actually singing ; concentrate all your attention on the sounds which you are producing, and let your breath take care of itself. Should your breathing become difficult, inhale gently, and let out the breath with a slow sigh. Do this a few times, and the tension will disappear.

Deep breathing, apart from its value in singing, tones and braces up the whole nervous system, and is one of the most effective remedies for nervousness.

When you have learned how to take breath, you must learn when and where to take it. Many singers make the mistake of trying to sing as long as they can in one breath, with complete disregard for the phrasing of the music. You should never attempt to sing in one breath more than you can comfortably manage. And when you want to take a fresh breath, you should do so at a place where there is a slight pause in the words. Such a pause will usually be found to coincide with a punctuation mark, but even if it does not, you should be able to decide from the sense of the words the proper place to take a breath.

You need not, of course, wait until your breath is nearly exhausted before you take another breath. In a phrase like this :

" How young, how fair, how beautiful ! "

the sense of the words is best conveyed by taking a breath at each comma. There will not be time for you to fill the lungs completely at each comma, so you should take what is known as a " half-breath," in which only a little breath is taken in. Sometimes it is necessary to *snatch* as quick a breath as possible in the middle of a long phrase, such as a Handelian run which is vocalised on a vowel sound ; here the breath must be taken where it interferes least with the musical phrasing.

Personality in Solo Singing

A perfectly trained voice, and the ability to pronounce words clearly and accurately, does not always

G

make a fine singer ; before a singer can merit such a description he must add to these attributes that subtle, indefinable thing—personality.

Personality is really a kind of persuasion ; the accomplished singer by singing a song in a certain way persuades his audience to like it. The singer with personality, like a good salesman, knows all the tricks of the trade, and by presenting his goods in the most attractive way, is able to sell them to his audience.

The old singing masters used to spend hours a week teaching their pupils deportment ; how to walk on to a stage, how to acknowledge applause, and how to beguile the audience with a smile. But when broadcasting was invented the singer, now invisible to his audience, could no longer rely on deportment to help him ; and the only way in which he could reach his unseen listeners was by infusing his personality into his song.

Whether you are singing before a live audience or before a live microphone, you must remember that it is impossible to make your audience feel what you do not feel yourself. And though a singer who is known to be a great artist may sometimes be forgiven for displaying affectation, or even insincerity on occasions, any lesser person will hardly be excused.

In order to give a sincere interpretation of a song, you must first understand it. It is not at all unusual to find that a singer who has been studying a song for some weeks does not even know the meaning of the words. It is obvious that until you appreciate the significance and the beauty of the words and music, you will not be able to convey these things to an audience.

When you are studying the words of a new song, read them through a few times, until you have grasped their meaning and the spirit in which they were written. Then go through them again, looking out for the subtler points which you probably missed in the first few readings. Decide which syllables and words should be emphasized and which passed over lightly, and whether any of the vowels should be lingered over, even ever so slightly, so as to convey the meaning of the words a little more clearly.

Consider the following line :

" A little *shiv'ring* bird that sings upon a tree."

A good artist would make his audience see and feel the shivering of the bird, by the gentlest pressure, and by lingering for a fraction of a second, upon the word " shiv'ring." A little more emphasis, a longer pause, and the effect would be ruined.

Such subtleties and fine shades of expression are only to be acquired by practice and experience, and if they do not come as quickly as you would wish, do not lose heart. Try to create something out of each song that you study, saturate yourself in the words and the music, learn all you can from the great artists, and you will soon find that your singing is being vitalized and enriched by the gain of personality.

Choral Singing

Choral singing, whether in a church choir or in a choral society, is excellent practice for the solo singer. He gains confidence from hearing other people's voices around him, and given a good choirmaster or conductor, he will learn a great deal about interpretation, and music in general.

Choral singing is easier than solo singing, so far as technique is concerned, but the singer who wishes to be a useful member of a choir should devote some time to the study of sight-reading.

The most important thing in choral singing is

unanimity of movement, which means that all the voices must attack or release a note, and swell or diminish the tone, exactly together. This unanimity must also be applied to words. Everyone must use the same vowel sounds, and there must be agreement on the pronunciation of any difficult words.

Choral music is usually written in four choral parts, (soprano, contralto, tenor, and bass), the mezzo-sopranos singing with the sopranos, and the baritones with the basses. These parts are sometimes subdivided, either temporarily or throughout the movement, into two parts. If the soprano part is divided, the sopranos sing the upper notes and the mezzo-sopranos the lower notes ; if the bass part is divided, the baritones sing the upper notes and the basses the lower notes.

Choral music written for male voices only is usually in four parts, for first and second tenors, and first and second basses. There is also some charming music in two, three, and four parts, for female voices.

When choral music is sung by voices alone, without the accompaniment of piano, organ, or orchestra, the balance of the voices becomes of supreme importance. Ideally, each section of the choir should be perfectly proportioned : in a choir of forty singers, for instance, there might be thirteen sopranos, eight contraltos, eight tenors, and eleven basses. But since contraltos and tenors are rarer than sopranos and basses, they will seldom be apportioned in this way, and there will probably be too many sopranos and too few contraltos and tenors. Good balance must then be obtained by grading the tone so that the weaker sections are not overwhelmed by the stronger sections. The standard of balance must always be the strength of the weakest part.

Interest in choral singing has been greatly stimulated by the Competition Festivals which are held each year in many parts of the country. These festivals provide small choirs with an incentive to study, and an opportunity of taking part, with other choirs, in performances of good music, under the direction of well-known professional conductors. The competitive element, too, is valuable, for it sets a standard of achievement which, though high, is reached by a great many amateur choirs.

Some Useful Exercises

(1) Here is an exercise in breath control and the production of pure vowel sounds. Practise each line of vowels separately. First speak the vowels in front of a mirror, so that you can watch the movement of the lips. Then sing them quite softly, taking a tiny breath before each note.

```
oo   oh   ah   ay   ee
ah   ay   ee   ay   ah
```

(2) These exercises are intended to be spoken. If they are practised conscientiously, they will help to produce a clear, crisp enunciation of the consonants.

(1) Bert brought back best butter.
(2) Please pay poor Peter promptly.
(3) Dan drowned Dora's din.
(4) Jean joined jolly Jack Jones.
(5) Tiny Tim's tart tastes tart.
(6) Fanny found five fine feathers.
(7) Ladies like light lunches.
(8) Charles chose cheap charms.

Double Consonants

(1) Dick calls Stephen names.

(2) Horace sells splendid doughnuts.
(3) Which church chimes sound?
(4) Bright ties suit Tim.

Further Study

Exercises and scales will help to increase the range, flexibility, and general control of the voice, and you should practise them every day. Do not practise for more than ten minutes at a time in the early stages, and do not try to master the exercises too quickly. There is a book called *Voice Placing and Training Exercises*, by George Dodds (Oxford University Press), which contains a carefully graded series of progressive exercises, which you will find most helpful. There are two editions, one for sopranos and tenors, the other for contraltos and basses.

When you are choosing your first solo, make sure that it is in a suitable key, and that the compass is not too wide for you. Most songs are published in two or more different keys; the compass is printed on the copy, so that you should have no difficulty in choosing the most suitable key.

CHAPTER X

HOW TO PRACTISE

We make music because we love it, so why should the practice and perfection of something we love become a drudgery. The truth is that practice is a pleasure only so long as it does not become a mechanical process. Nowadays life has so many distractions that concentration, especially in our leisure hours, is becoming more and more difficult. Often we try to do two things at once, and do neither of them well. We read a book in the train, and listen to the conversation of our fellow passengers at the same time. We write a letter while the radio is blaring. And we only half do each of these things. So it is little wonder that when we want to concentrate all our attention on something, we have to make a conscious effort.

We sit down at the piano, or take up the violin, with every intention of putting in an hour's solid practice. We play a scale or two, and then start on some exercise or other. And suddenly our mind wanders ; we look out of the window and see the neighbour's cat climbing over the fence, and wonder how the kittens are getting on, and then we remember a letter which we have forgotten to post, and decide that we have done enough practice for the day.

The real difference between a great musical artist and an indifferent amateur is not that one has greater musical ability than the other ; it is simply that the artist knows how to develop his ability to the full, and the amateur does not. The old misquotation " Genius is an infinite capacity for taking pains " is trite but true.

Practice which consists of the mechanical rattling off

of scales and exercises is not merely a waste of time ; it is definitely harmful. Practice makes perfect, but aimless practice only develops and perfects the faults of the player. Repetition is valuable only if there is reason behind it. Every time you repeat anything ask yourself " What fault am I trying to overcome by this repetition ? "

There is one excellent way of developing concentration, and that is to read music at sight. It is almost impossible to read unfamiliar music if the attention is wandering. So be sure to include sight-reading in your practice.

Learn to practise one thing at a time. Concentrate on each point of technique separately ; if you are a pianist, on accuracy, fingering, pedalling, and phrasing : if you are a singer, on breathing, diction, resonance, interpretation ; and so on.

Practise in sections ; isolate the difficult passages and work at them one at a time. Try to spot the difficulty and to devise a remedy. Suppose, for example, that you are playing a scale passage, and you find that the third finger of your left hand is inclined to play its note a little before the other fingers, making the passage uneven. If you simply repeat the passage several times without thought, there will probably be no improvement at all ; the fault, in fact, is likely to be aggravated. But if when you practise the passage you deliberately pause on the offending note, so that instead of being too quick it is rather too slow, the fault will gradually be eliminated. You see the idea ? This principle of anthithesis may frequently be applied to faults and bad habits, with encouraging results.

Practise as regularly as you can. Try to put in some practice every day, even if only for ten minutes. If you can spare, say, an hour a day, you should divide it fairly evenly between (1) scales and exercises ; (2) solos ; (3) sight-reading and ear-training.

Do not be discouraged if you do not seem to be making sufficient progress. The strange thing about practising is that although improvement is gradual it does not always appear to be so ; you may sometimes practise a passage for several days without making any perceptible progress, and then suddenly find that you have mastered it.

Never practise so long that you lose interest in what you are doing, and never practise when you are physically or mentally tired. Practice is, or should be, a step towards the greater enjoyment of music, so make it a pleasure in itself.

Training the Memory

The development of a reliable musical memory is a necessity for the solo pianist, string player, or singer, who wishes to perform in public. Convention demands that he should play without music, although, curiously enough, the organist is seldom expected to play from memory, and a performer in an orchestra or string quartet is always allowed to have his music before him.

The faculty for memorizing music varies greatly in the individual, and is not necessarily conditioned by musical ability. Some musicians find difficulty in remembering even the simplest piece, while others are capable of prodigious feats of memory. Tausig, one of the world's greatest pianists, was able to play from memory every piece of importance in the repertory of the piano.

Memory implies two things : the capacity to retain knowledge, and the power to recall it. The accuracy with which we retain knowledge depends on how deeply it impresses us. The things we find easiest to remember are those which interest us the most. The association of ideas also helps us to remember. Coleridge, in his *Biographia Literaria*, gives a good example of this. " Seeing," he says, " a mackerel, it may happen that I immediately think of gooseberries, because I, at one time, ate mackerel, with gooseberries as the sauce ; the first syllable of the latter word being that which had co-existed with the image of the bird so called, I may then think of a goose. In the next moment, the image of a swan may rise before me, though I had never seen the two birds together."

Because of this principle of association, facts which bear some relation to each other are more easily remembered than those which are disconnected. It follows, then, that when we want to memorize a piece of music, we should try to determine the relationship between the parts of which it is made up.

Memory for music depends upon three forms of perception ; visual, aural, and tactile.

Some people are gifted with very great powers of visual perception, and are able to see a page of music, or even a page of a railway time-table, in their mind's eye, and to reproduce it with complete accuracy. This really amounts to mental photography, and is often accomplished without conscious effort. Others, who are less gifted, will find that music is easier to visualize if the shape is first concentrated upon, before dissecting it into sections. When the general shape has been memorized, the music should be carefully analysed. Points to look for are (1) the pattern of the melody, harmony, and fingering ; (2) whether any passages are repeated ; (3) which passages are based upon some familiar figure, such as a scale passage, or an arpeggio.

Aural perception is the most important constituent of musical memory, and it may be developed by careful ear-training. The ear, like the eye, should be trained to take in the general design of the music, as well as the details.

Tactile perception means that the player is able to memorize the *feel* of the fingers as they play. Practice with closed eyes (advocated in the next section, as an aid to sight-reading) will help the player to feel his way about. The string player should notice which of his fingers are closer together than the others when playing a particular passage, and where any big stretches occur. The singer need not concern himself with tactile perception, but he should learn to memorize the sensations which he feels when he is producing the right kind of tone.

Nervousness often makes memorizing difficult, and causes memory failure. Too much conscious effort sometimes has the effect of paralysing the memory ; we have all tried to recall a word which is on the tip of our tongue, but somehow eludes us. It is often better to play or sing the music through, noting the various points, without *trying* to memorize it, but repeating it at intervals. Many actors and actresses adopt this method when studying their parts.

Memory failure, when it is caused through nervousness, is usually due either to self-consciousness or to the knowledge that the music has been insufficiently prepared. Most performers are self-conscious when they appear in public for the first time ; the cure is deep breathing before the performance, and concentration on the music, and not on the audience, during the performance. The cure for unpreparedness is an obvious one.

Learning to Read at Sight

The ability to read music at sight is all the more valuable because many amateur and professional performers are bad sight-readers. Sight-reading is a natural gift to the extent that it presents little difficulty to some

people, even though they may be indifferent performers ;
but those who are not so gifted should be encouraged to
practise assiduously, for by doing so they will develop
what ability they have to at least a useful standard of
competence.

The solo pianist, if he is a bad sight-reader, may not
find that he is unduly handicapped, but the accompanist
who cannot read at sight will be able to make very little
progress. The string or wind player, when he plays in an
orchestra, is frequently called upon to play at sight.
Many singers are notoriously bad sight-readers, and learn
their songs by banging out the notes with one finger on
the piano, a method which is both inartistic and
laborious.

It may seem scarcely necessary to say that the first
thing you must do on being given a piece of music to
read at sight is to look at the key and time signatures.
Yet it is astonishing how many people fail to do this, and
find, to their confusion, that they have started the movement in, say, E Major, when the key signature is E flat
major, or that they are trying to play in a major instead
of a minor key.

A movement with a key signature of two sharps
may, of course, be in D major or in B minor, and if you
have any doubts it is best to look at the last bars of the
movement, which will almost always provide the clue.
If the movement ends in B minor, you may be pretty
certain that it begins in the same key.

The next point, which applies particularly to
pianists and organists, and, to a lesser degree, to string
and wind players, is that you cannot look at the music
and your hands at the same time. You must, therefore,
be able to find the notes easily and accurately, without
having to glance at the fingers. It is good practice to
close your eyes, name any note at random, and then try

to play it. You will probably find this difficult at first, but if you persevere you will soon make good progress.

A special difficulty of the pianist is to find the notes of a chord without glancing at the keyboard. It may be overcome if the fingers are first placed correctly upon the keys, and the *feel* of the chord memorised. The fingers should then be lifted from the keyboard, and the chord played with the eyes closed. Practice in finding notes on the keyboard of the piano, or on the fingerboard of a string instrument, is of great value even if music is not to be read at sight, for it enables the notes to be played with greater precision and confidence.

The ear plays as important a part as the eye in sight-reading, and it cannot be too highly trained. Practice in singing melodies and tapping rhythms is especially useful.

When you are playing at sight, it is important that you should keep strictly to the time and rhythm of the music. If you do this, you will not be able to stop every time you make a mistake, but you should remember where the mistakes occur. When you have finished the movement, return to the difficult passages, and practise them separately until the faults have been overcome.

You should be able to find plenty of material for sight-reading. Any unfamiliar piece will serve, but remember that it should not be too difficult, or contain any technical problems which are likely to distract your attention. What you must aim at is *accuracy* ; however simple the music, however slow the time, get the notes and the rhythm right. And do not forget to watch the phrasing and expression marks, and to try to capture the mood in which the piece is written.

The key signatures of the music should be varied as much as possible, so that you will be able to read in any key with equal facility. Even a few minutes a day devoted to sight-reading will pay rich dividends.

CHAPTER XI

LISTENING AND LEARNING

Making the Most of Music

When we read a fine passage of prose, such as Lytton Strachey's description of the passing of Queen Victoria, we do so with one of two purposes in view. We may read simply for enjoyment, for the pleasure of having the emotions agreeably aroused. Or we may read with a view to discovering where the strength and beauty of the passage lies, so that we, too, may learn to write good prose.

We listen to music in exactly the same way, and if we want to turn our listening to good account, we must understand what we hear, and analyse such points as we are anxious to master. As musical performers we must have a measure for perfection, a yard-stick with which we can determine our progress.

We shall find such a measure by listening to the performance of those artists who are acknowledged to be great. Nowadays we have plenty of opportunities, for even if we cannot go to concerts, we can still listen to the radio or the gramophone. We can, of course, learn more from concert-going, for by seeing the performer we can notice what he does with his hands and his feet, or, if he is singing, with his lips and his breath. But even when the performance comes to us through the medium of the radio or the gramophone, these processes may often be reconstructed with a reasonable degree of accuracy.

If we listen to learn how to measure our progress, in other words, to learn how to listen to ourselves, we must make full use of our critical faculties. It is not enough to accept as perfect everything that we hear performed by a great artist. Many geniuses have eccentricities and mannerisms which amateurs often mistake for virtues and try to imitate. And even a consummate performer has his " off " days when he and his playing are flat and uninspired.

The way to make the most of a concert or a recital, whether at a concert hall or on the radio, is to study the programme beforehand. You may find that some of the music to be performed is well within your powers. If so, listen carefully, and mark all the points as they occur to you : tempo, interpretation, phrasing, pedalling (piano), bowing (string instruments), and breathing (singing). Then tackle the music yourself. Buy a record, or hear it on the radio. Do this with several pieces, and you will soon find that your powers of observation have been so developed that you are able to analyse the principles of good performance. And once learned, those principles may be applied to any music whatsoever.

It is not a bad plan sometimes to listen to indifferent performers (there should be no dearth of opportunities). This will teach you how *not* to do it, and will help you to diagnose your own faults.

The Art of Musical Appreciation

Music cannot be divided into a series of water-tight compartments. Your capacity for enjoyment should not be restricted to such music as you yourself are able to perform. You, as a pianist or a violinist, cannot afford to turn a deaf ear to the singer, the flautist, or the orchestra.

The more you can learn about those kinds of music-making that are as yet unfamiliar to you, the more you will be able to appreciate music. You should certainly know something about the orchestra. For the orchestra is the finest instrument (if we may regard it as an instrument) of all, and is capable of the greatest variety of tone-colour and expression.

By far the best way of listening to orchestral music is to follow the full score (for an explanation, see Chapter XII). Full scores of all the best-known orchestral works may be obtained in miniature form for a small sum. With a little practice you will be able to follow the music in the score, at the same time as you hear it played. And if you study beforehand, you can form your own impression of the music, and test its accuracy when the orchestra translates it into sound.

Learning from Radio, Gramophone, and Tape Recorder

There is no doubt that the invention of the gramophone and the radio, though it may have diverted some people from music-making, has proved a great boon to musicians. Yet many people do not realize the possibilities of these instruments as aids to musical study.

The radio has greater limitations than the gramophone, because it is necessary to plan listening well ahead, whereas a record is always at hand and may be repeated at will. It has already been suggested that you should study, by means of the radio or of a record, music which you will afterwards be able to perform yourself. But have you ever thought of performing *with* the gramophone?

Suppose you are a pianist. You buy a record, played by some great soloist, of a piano piece which you are studying. You practise until you can play it reasonably well. Then you set the record going and, sitting at the piano, go through the motions of playing, without actually pressing down the keys. You then repeat the record, and this time you find that you are able to play as you listen to it. After a few more attempts, you will be able to follow the artist's interpretation of the piece almost exactly. What more instructive and enjoyable way of learning to play can there be! You must, of course, make sure that your piano is the same pitch as the record. You will remember that the pitch of a record may be raised or lowered by increasing or slackening the speed.

If you are a string or wind player, you can practise in the same way. If you are a singer, you can either buy a record by a well-known singer (make sure that it is in the right key for your voice), or one of those special records which consist of the piano accompaniment to a popular song, to which you supply the vocal line.

Playing or singing with the radio is a little more difficult, though by no means impossible. It is just a matter of planning well ahead. All music on the radio is played in concert pitch, so if your instrument is tuned to this pitch you need not worry on that score. But you cannot be certain that a song will be sung in any particular key; you will, naturally, choose a programme which is sung by a singer with the same kind of voice as your own.

The tape recorder offers unique opportunities for self-criticism, since the instrumentalist or singer is able, by recording and listening back to his own performance, to make a note of his weak points, and of the progress he has made since his previous attempts.

What is this Chamber Music?

Chamber music, to some, is the purest form of musical art; to others, it is just an excuse for turning off the radio. The chief reason for this difference of opinion is that few people know exactly what chamber music is; and, as they have a vague feeling that it is rather "highbrow" and dull, they never bother to find out.

Until the seventeenth century, when the first public

concerts were given, public musical performances took place in churches, in theatres, or in the palaces of royalty and the halls of the aristocracy. These latter performances, whether vocal or instrumental, were distinguished from those which took place in the church or theatre by the term "chamber music", and a musician who held a position in a noble household was given the title of *musico da camera* (chamber musician).

Nowadays, chamber music has come to mean any serious instrumental (but not vocal) music of two or more parts, in which each part is played by a single instrument. Thus, a duet for violin and piano, a trio for violin, 'cello and piano, a quartet for two violins, viola and 'cello, and a sextet for two violins two violas, and two 'cellos, all come within the term chamber music.

By far the most important combination is the string quartet. Each of the four parts, first violin, second violin, viola and 'cello, is of equal importance. Each player should be a soloist, yet each must blend with the other.

The string quartet, heard for the first time, often strikes the listener as rather colourless, and lacking in strong emotion. The truth is that this music is different from any other, and is therefore frequently misunderstood. It is subtle, intimate music; it lacks the big *crescendos* and climaxes to be found in orchestral music, which relies for much of its effect on the duplication, in mass, of the tone of string instruments. The players in the string quartet are individualists; they have no conductor to direct their performance, and they have no leader. Their playing is merged into what is called a good *ensemble* (which means that they play well together) by a kind of mental autonomy. The four players, through long association, acquire a mutual understanding which enables them to achieve perfect co-ordination.

Chamber music for fewer than four strings is not common, although there are a number of trios, either for two violins and 'cello, or for violin, viola and 'cello. Some of these are quite easy to play, and very suitable for amateur performance.

The addition of the piano to a chamber combination adds a new kind of tone-colour. The chief combinations which include piano are the piano quartet (the string trio with the piano added), and the piano quintet (the string quartet with the piano added).

Most of the great masters wrote a good deal of chamber music, and there is a wide repertory, both classical and modern, to choose from. If you are listening to chamber music for the first time, you might start with some of the more popular works like Haydn's *Emperor* Quartet, Tschaikovsky's Quartet in D Major (Op. II), or Schubert's *Trout* Quintet.

If you are a pianist, or a string player, why not start a chamber combination; a string or piano quartet, or a piano quintet? An advertisement in a local paper will often bring replies from suitable players.

Chamber music is the ideal form of home music-making, and, without a doubt, the perfect medium for musical expression.

CHAPTER XII

THE RISE OF THE ORCHESTRA

If you have been to a symphony concert at the Albert Hall, you will probably agree that the scene is an impressive one. Masses of violins, rows of violas, 'cellos, basses, wood-wind and brass instruments crowd the platform; at the back are the kettledrums and the other percussion instruments; in front there are a couple of harps. All the players are busy blowing, piping, plucking and tuning their instruments. The conductor enters amidst applause. As he raises his baton the medley of sounds dies away, and the great hall is silent. The orchestra waits, instruments raised, bows poised, lips and fingers ready. The audience sits very still, watching the conductor's arm. Down it comes, and the violins swing into a melody, the wood-wind and brass combine in rich harmonies, the cymbals clash, there is a sweep of harps, and the pattern of the music begins to unfold itself.

When you listen to a modern symphony orchestra, you may sometimes wonder why this particular combination of instruments should produce the best results, and how all the instruments were brought together.

How the Orchestra Began

The idea of combining different groups of instruments to form an orchestra was probably thought of soon after the instruments themselves were invented. The earliest performers, no doubt, soon discovered that it was more enjoyable if several of them played their primitive instruments together; the result must have been so crude that if it could be heard to-day it would be quite unintelligible to modern ears.

The ancient Greeks had string and wind instruments ; the principal ones were the lyre, a kind of harp with four strings, and the flute. The Romans used wind instruments made of wood and brass for directing troop movements and providing military music. But though these primitive orchestras existed, it was not until centuries later that the modern orchestra began to take shape.

By the beginning of the sixteenth century a large number of string and wind instruments were in use ; viols of several sizes (from which the present string family is descended), flutes, oboes, trumpets, trombones, and drums. In the golden age of Queen Elizabeth the orchestra came into its own. The queen, who was herself an accomplished musician, had her own orchestra of some fifty players. The technique of the string instruments was now beginning to be established, but the wood-wind and brass instruments were still very imperfect. Some of the orchestral effects which the composers of this period demanded were fantastic ; they included the use of giant double-basses, bombs and cannons.

The first orchestral score of any real importance is that of Monterverdi's *Orfeo* (1607). Monterverdi's orchestra consisted of some forty musicians. About seventeen of these played viols of various sizes ; the others played flutes, oboes, trumpets, trombones, harps, harpsichords and organs.

From Bach to Mozart

By the early eighteenth century the orchestra had made further progress. Instruments had been improved, and new ways of combining them had been worked out. Technique had also advanced. Some of the high trumpet passages to be found in Bach's orchestral scores are outside the capacity of average modern players, and how they could have been played in his time remains a mystery. The most likely explanation is that certain trumpet players of the period specialized in the performance of high passages, which in time became easy to them.

Bach had a large number of instruments at his disposal. He did not use all of them in the same score, but selected those which he thought most suitable for each work, usually including a keyboard instrument, such as the harpsichord or the clavichord.

It was not until late in the eighteenth century, the time of Haydn and Mozart, that the combination of the orchestra became more or less standardised. Haydn and Mozart may be said to have established the principles of modern orchestration. The orchestra in Haydn's time usually consisted of between thirty and forty players. Here is the instrumentation of one of Haydn's symphonies, the *London*, in D major :

> Two Flutes
> Two Oboes
> Two Clarinets
> Two Bassoons
> Two Horns
> Two Trumpets
> Timpani (two drums)
> 1st Violins
> 2nd Violins
> Violas
> 'Cellos
> Basses

Trombones were never included in the symphonies of either Haydn or Mozart, but they were occasionally used in other works. Haydn made more use of the clarinets than Mozart, who left them out of many of his symphonies, or used them in place of oboes.

The Orchestra Grows

Several of the principles upon which modern orchestration is founded were, by this time, firmly established. In Bach's period many of the wind instruments were used merely to double the string parts, but in Haydn's orchestra the wind and string instruments were regarded as independent of one another. Either group could play on its own, and if the two groups were used together they could, if desired, play in contrasted rhythms. But it was left to Beethoven to perfect these new principles.

So we find that orchestration is becoming more and more flexible ; and new instruments are gradually making their appearance. In Beethoven's 9th Symphony (*The Choral*), which he wrote between 1817 and 1823, he requires, in addition to the instruments in Haydn's orchestra, a piccolo, a double-bassoon, two extra horns (making four in all), three trombones, and three extra percussion instruments, the triangle, the cymbals, and the bass drum.

The technique of the instruments in Beethoven's time was still a good way from approaching modern standards. Trumpets and horns were not yet fitted with valves, so that they could play only a limited series of notes. Horn players, instead of using one crook as they do to-day, were provided with an armful, which they changed according to the key of the music.

The Modern Symphony Orchestra

Modern orchestration may be said to date from the beginning of the nineteenth century, that is from the time of Berlioz and Wagner. The ideas which these two composers put into practice were revolutionary. Under their influence the orchestra grew by leaps and bounds. Berlioz's ideas on orchestration were gigantic. In his treatise on the subject he gives the combination of what he considers to be the ideal orchestra. It consists of 240 strings, thirty grand pianos, thirty harps, and wind and percussion on a similar scale. Berlioz once engaged an orchestra of 600 players for a concert of his music at the Paris Opera. Though Wagner's orchestration was a little less ambitious, *The Ring of the Nibelungs* requires an orchestra of over a hundred players, including eight horns, five tubas, and six harps.

These huge forces enabled many new varieties of tone colour to be introduced into the orchestra, although, for reasons of economy, some works are now played by a considerably smaller number of players than that demanded in the scores.

The average symphony orchestra of to-day, when its full complement is used, numbers from eighty to a hundred players. The combination of an orchestra of eighty would be on these lines:

	Players
First Violins	14
Second Violins	12
Violas	10
'Cellos	8
Double-Basses	8
Flutes	2
Piccolo	1
Oboes	2
Cor Anglais	1
Clarinets	2
Bass Clarinet	1
Bassoons	2
Double Bassoon	1
Horns	4
Trumpets	3
Trombones	3

Tuba	..	..	..	1
Timpani..	..	..	..	1
Percussion	..	..	..	3
Harp	..	..	..	1

80

What is Orchestration ?

When a composer is writing a symphony or other big orchestral work, he usually arranges it for orchestra as he goes along. When he does this he is said to be making a full score, that is, a score containing the exact notes that each instrument is to play. The copyist then copies out the parts for the instruments, and the score is afterwards used by the conductor of the orchestra, who is able to see at a glance what notes each instrument ought to be playing.

Each instrumental part is usually written on a separate stave, and these staves are arranged in a special order so that they may be easily read. The instruments of the orchestra are divided into four groups, strings, wood-wind, brass, and percussion ; the harp, if used, is regarded as an additional instrument. The wood-wind group is usually written at the top of the page, then come the brass, percussion and harp, and finally the strings at the foot of the page. This is the order in which the page is arranged :

Piccolo
Two Flutes
Two Oboes
Cor Anglais   } Wood-wind Group
Two Clarinets
Bass Clarinet
Two Bassoons
Double-Bassoon

Four French Horns ⎫
Three Trumpets   ⎪
Three Trombones   ⎬ Brass Group
Bass Tuba   ⎭

Timpani   ⎫
Percussion Instruments   ⎪
   (Bass Drum, Side Drum,   ⎬ Percussion Group
   Cymbals, Glockenspiel,   ⎪
   Triangle, Bells, Tam-   ⎪
   bourine, etc.)   ⎭

Harp

1st Violins   ⎫
2nd Violins   ⎪
Violas   ⎬ String Group
'Cellos   ⎪
Double-Basses   ⎭

The orchestrator may treat these four groups in several different ways. They may all play together in the same rhythm, the wood-wind, brass, and string groups each forming complete harmony. That is to say that if any one group were to play alone, the effect would be satisfying to the ear. Now let us see what happens when the three groups are blended, and the percussion group added. If the music is loud, the brass will easily be the most powerful group. The wood-wind will add brilliance to the brass, and will also fill in the upper octaves. The strings will help to bind the wood-wind and brass together, and will take some of the edge off the brass, and make them sound more mellow. The percussion group will add rhythm to the music.

Now let us suppose that the music is soft instead of loud. The strings will now be the most powerful group, the wood-wind will add colour and brightness, the brass will add body and the percussion will add rhythm as before.

But the composer will not let all the instruments in the orchestra play all the time ; if he did he would soon bore his listeners. And he will not use his brass and percussion too often, for these instruments are like scarlet on a painter's palette ; a touch here and there is exciting, but a splash of colour quickly loses its appeal. So the composer will employ the more delicate colours for his background, using the strings most of the time, adding his wood-wind and horns now and then, and keeping his brass, his drums, and his cymbals, for his high spots and climaxes.

Sometimes, for a change of colour, he will let the wood-wind or the brass group play alone, and he will often use his wood-wind and horns for solo passages, accompanied by the strings. A charming example of this occurs in the second movement of the *Unfinished Symphony* by Schubert. Here the same phrase is played, first by the clarinet, then by the oboe, and finally by the flute. The delicate contrast of tone-colour is delightful, but must be heard to be appreciated.

The Personality of the Conductor

Nowadays, people who go to concerts are as much interested in the conductor as in the music which is to be played. So one conductor's "reading" of Mozart or Beethoven may be preferred to another's, just as the interpretation by a particular pianist of some favourite piece may be considered the best.

Conducting, as we know it, is little more than a century old, and though it was practised long before this, it amounted to little more than the beating of time, to keep a body of musicians or singers together. There were several methods of marking the beats; sometimes they were shown by the waving of a handkerchief or of a roll of paper, sometimes by the thumping of a heavy stick on the floor. This audible method of time-beating must have been rather disconcerting for the musicians. There is a story, which may or may not be true, that the composer Lulli died of a wound in his foot, which he accidentally inflicted on himself while conducting in this way.

In time the visual and audible ways of beating were replaced by a "conductor", who presided over the orchestra while sitting at the keyboard (harpsichord, piano, or organ) at the same time filling in any harmony that might be missing. Later the violin-conductor came into being, conducting the orchestra with his bow, and playing at intervals. Eventually the bow gave way to the baton, which was at first a heavy stick, often fixed to the conductor's wrist by a strap so that it should not fly out of his hand and injure someone.

So the idea of the conductor as an interpreter was born, and the art of the conductor developed to such an extent that to-day the attributes which he ought to possess are far more numerous than those required of any player in the orchestra.

The conductor does much of his work at rehearsals, though in this country he is allowed far too few of them. He must know how to get the best out of his players ; he must understand the capabilities of every orchestral instrument, and he should be able to play several of them ; he must display unfailing tact and good humour, and keep his temper in sometimes difficult circumstances. He must know what the composer wants and see that he gets it ; he must be able to interpret music of every age and of every nationality ; and above all, he must possess a personality which will make itself felt in everything to which he sets his hand.

CHAPTER XIII

THE ROMANCE OF MUSIC

The Beginnings of Music

Music, like all other arts, is chiefly derived from the ancients, but no one can say exactly how it began. Primitive man, no doubt, soon began to discover that he could express his anger, his fear, and his other emotions by the use of his voice. This may have led him to the discovery of vocal music. The song of the birds may have helped him also, for it is well known that the blackbird's song consists of true musical intervals.

We know that *our* music dates back only about 1,200 years ; even then it took nearly 1,000 years to develop. The reason why music was not developed as quickly as the other arts is probably because sculpture and painting are imitative arts, but music is not. Primitive man had plenty of models to imitate when he wished to chisel images on the walls of his caves ; but, except for the song of the birds, he could find nothing to imitate when he wished to make music.

The first traces of music were discovered in Asia, the " cradle of human culture," and in Africa. The Egyptians, in particular, possessed musical instruments capable of a wide range of expression. Yet even if these instruments had been preserved in perfect condition we should still have little idea of the kind of music that was played on them, for the ancients had no system of musical notation and their music was played or sung entirely by ear.

Some very early examples of Chinese music exist, and it is known that the Chinese played a number of different instruments. One of the most interesting is the " King," which is said to have existed in 2,300 B.C. It consists of a number of stones of different sizes, suspended in rows, and struck with a wooden mallet. Though Western music has developed very rapidly during the last few centuries, Chinese music has changed but little. To our ears it sounds completely crude, because we are quite unable to understand it. In the same way, our modern music leaves the Chinaman quite unmoved, though his own music may deeply affect him.

Music, for the Greeks, meant any art over which the nine Muses presided, and included painting, sculpture, and poetry, which was set to music and sung. Many of the Greek philosophers made a profound study of music. Aristotle, in particular, recognised that music is not a diversion in itself but an ennobling influence, and he denounced bad and effeminate music.

Music and the Bible

There are many interesting references in the Bible to music and musical instruments. In the Book of Genesis, iv, 21, we read that Jubal was " the father of all such as handle the harp and the organ," and he may, therefore, be said to be the inventor of stringed and wind instruments. Moses was a musician, and in Numbers x, we find his directions for the making of two silver trumpets, which are to be fashioned from one piece of metal, and are to be used to give signals to the children of Israel during their wanderings in the desert. These instruments must have been large and powerful.

In Exodus xv, 20, Miriam, the prophetess, " took a timbrel in her hand ; and all the women went out after her with timbrels and with dances." A timbrel is an ancient kind of tambourine, and the one that Miriam used was probably a kind of drum fitted with metal jingles, and not unlike the tambourine of to-day. Miriam was accompanied with timbrels when she sung her triumphal song of victory, which Handel has immortalised in his final chorus to *Israel in Egypt*.

David, who was an accomplished musician as well as an inspired poet, was the inventor or maker of a large number of musical instruments. In I Chronicles xxiii, 5, " four thousand praised the Lord " with the instruments which David had made. David was a skilled harpist, and we are told in the Old Testament that he used to play to Saul, and that his playing soothed the King, and banished his evil thoughts.

Solomon, too, formed bands of musicians, and choirs of female vocalists who probably performed secular music in his harem. The Song of Solomon was almost certainly intended to be sung to music, for it is clearly written in lyrical form.

It is evident that choral singing by mixed choirs was practised, for there are many biblical references to singing-men and singing women. And in 2 Ecclesiastes, ii, 8, we read " I gat me men singers and women singers, and the delights of the sons of men, as musical instruments and that of all sorts."

The psaltery, which is mentioned in the Bible, is one of the earliest stringed instruments, and is played by plucking the strings with a plectrum, or with the fingers. The cornet (" David played before the Lord on cornets." 2 Samuel vi, 5), bears no resemblance to the modern instrument, and is, in fact, a form of the ancient " cornett," which is a brass instrument with finger holes, and, therefore, has an affinity to both wood-wind and brass instruments. Other instruments mentioned in the Bible are the viol, the flute, the dulcimer (a psaltery which is played with hammers instead of with the fingers), the cymbals, the tabret (a kind of tambourine), and the pipes, which may have been similar to the ancient " pipes of pan."

Although we read of " the melody of thy viols " (Amos v, 23), we find no mention of harmony in the Bible, for it had not yet been discovered.

The Birth of the Scale

Pythagoras, the Greek philosopher, who lived from about 570 to 500 B.C., was fond of experimenting with strings. He used to stretch them over a resonant box, and one day he discovered that by dividing a string in half he could raise the pitch an octave ; that by dividing it at the two-thirds he could raise it a perfect fifth ; and that by dividing it at the three-quarters he could raise it by a perfect fourth. This was an important musical discovery, but many centuries elapsed before it was developed.

During the fourth and sixth centuries, Ambrose, Bishop of Milan, and Pope Gregory, whose names give us Ambrosian and Gregorian Chant, devised eight different kinds of scale, now called " modes." The only mode that we recognise to-day is that formed by playing eight consecutive white keys on the piano, starting with C. The other modes may be heard by playing eight consecutive white keys, starting with D, E, F, G, A, and B. Some of these modes have been used by modern composers, Vaughan Williams in particular. They give the music a characteristic flavour.

By this time a form of musical notation was in existence in which dots and points were placed on seven parallel lines, but this could not have been very intelligible or easy to read. Then at the beginning of the eleventh century, a Benedictine monk called Guido set to work to improve the musical scale. He reduced the number of lines to four, and placed points not only *on*, but also *between* the lines. Guido's system, with certain modifications, is still in use to-day.

H

The invention of harmony was probably due to the introduction of the organ, which took place in France about 750, and which came to this country during the tenth century.

Bar-lines did not come into general use until the sixteenth century, and it may be interesting to mention that some modern composers have dispensed with them, feeling that the performer should not be committed to a rigid observance of musical accents. Clefs had to be devised when the compass of the melody became too big for the stave.

Our present system of notation is by no means ideal, especially as music tends to become more and more complex. In some modern piano music the performer is confronted with such a maze of accidentals that it would probably be easier to dispense with the key signature, which may, if contradicted often enough, actually increase the number of accidentals.

The Growth of Musical Form

All music has some kind of form. Look at this old Welsh melody.

ALL THROUGH THE NIGHT

You will see that it consists of sixteen bars. But there are actually only eight *different* bars, because the first four bars are repeated in bars five to eight, and again in bars thirteen to sixteen. If we call the first four bars A, and let B represent bars nine to twelve, we may express the form of the tune like this : A A B A.

If you play or sing this melody you will notice a falling off in flow and movement in bars three and four, seven and eight, and fifteen and sixteen. This falling off forms what is known as cadences, points of repose which serve very much the same purpose as punctuation marks in literature. They allow one, as it were, to take a fresh breath before going on. Some cadences, known as Full Closes, have a conclusive effect which may be compared to that of the full stop ; others, known as Half Closes, produce the effect of temporary repose, and correspond to the comma or semi-colon. Cadences divide a complete musical idea into smaller periods—sections (of two or more notes), phrases (of two or more sections), and sentences (of two or more phrases).

The form of modern instrumental music has been influenced by two basic ideas, from which the complex musical architecture we call by such names as the symphony, the sonata, and the overture has been developed. The first idea is exemplified in the national air *The Bailiff's Daughter of Islington* ; this tune naturally divides itself into two almost equal parts, A and B, and is said to be in Binary or two-part form. The second idea is exemplified in the tune *All Through the Night* which, as we have seen, consists of a statement, a repetition, a contrasting idea, and a restatement—in other words ‖:A:‖ B A ; this tune is said to be in Ternary or three-part form.

In discussing musical form it is necessary to consider modulation—the passing from one key to another during the course of a composition. Music which remains in one key for any length of time quickly becomes monotonous. It is therefore usual to find a piece moving temporarily to another key, or passing through several keys, before returning to the original one. Temporary modulation is usually effected by means of accidentals, the key-signature remaining unaltered. The most common modulation in simple music is to a key a fourth or a fifth higher (known as the subdominant and dominant keys) and back again. These keys are said to be " related " ; certain other keys, which have fewer notes in common, are said to be " unrelated."

The early instrumental compositions, such as the suites of Bach and Handel, were chiefly composed of dance movements. The eighteenth century saw the development of the " Sonata," the most important form in modern music. A sonata, as we use the word to-day, is a composition for one instrument alone, such as the piano or the organ, or for two instruments, such as the piano and violin. Sonatas for other combinations of instruments are called by different names. Those for three instruments are called " Trios " ; those for four, five, or six, " Quartets," " Quintets," " Sextets," and so on ; those for orchestra are called " Symphonies," and those for one or more solo instruments with orchestra " Concertos."

A Sonata is generally in three or four movements, and consists of :

1. A quick movement in " Sonata Form."
2. A slow movement of a song-like character.
3. A bright minuet or scherzo movement.
4. A lively movement.

A movement in Sonata Form, briefly, consists of three parts ; the " Exposition," in which the composer sets out his musical material, the " Development," in which he extends and develops his ideas, and the " Recapitulation," in which he restates his original ideas and brings the movement to a satisfactory conclusion.

Since the earliest days of instrumental music, the Variation Form has been popular with composers. In this form a short tune, which may or may not be original, is treated in a variety of ways, so that it appears each time in a different garb. This may be effected by clothing the tune with new harmony, by embellishing it with figures, or by any other means which an ingenious composer may devise.

The " Fugue," of which Bach was a master, is an instrumental or vocal composition in which a short tune, called the " subject," is announced by a single voice (or instrumental part), which is answered at a different pitch by a second voice, and so on.

The Classics and the Romantics

In 1685 Johann Sebastian Bach was born at Eisenach in Germany. He came from a long line of musicians ; the name of Bach, as cantor or organist, was familiar in many German churches. Bach had to earn his own living when he was fifteen, and as he was gifted with a beautiful voice he joined the choir of the convent school of St. Michael, at Luneburg. At eighteen he joined the Duke of Weimar's band as a violinist, and later became organist at Arnstadt, where he began to compose music for the church. The simple people of Arnstadt did not understand the strange harmonies which Bach introduced into his music, and before long he was severely reprimanded by the authorities for confusing the congregation.

Bach gave up his post at Arnstadt to become Court Organist to the Duke of Weimar, and later Musical Director to Prince Leopold. He was finally appointed organist at St. Thomas' Church at Leipzig, where he remained for twenty-seven years until his death in 1750.

Bach was widely known as the finest organist of his

time, but he received little recognition as a composer ; he lived a quiet, uneventful life, and unlike his great contemporary Handel he travelled very little. Bach was a prolific composer. His cantatas, sacred and secular, number many hundreds. His greatest choral works are the *B minor Mass* and the *St. Matthew Passion*.

Bach was a master of counterpoint and fugue. His *Forty-eight Preludes and Fugues* are some of the greatest musical treasures that we possess. His music may be said to form the backbone of the classical tradition.

Bach was followed by a succession of German composers. Gluck (1714–87) did much to reform the opera, and established a new relationship between the poetry and the music. Haydn and Mozart were the first to establish and perfect Sonata Form, and to bring to instrumental music the unity which it lacked. Both Haydn and Mozart were prolific symphonists ; between them they wrote nearly two hundred symphonies, of which some dozen or so are regularly performed to-day. Though Haydn had an Opera House at his disposal when he was musical director to Prince Esterhazy, he preferred to write instrumental music, especially for small chamber combinations, such as the string quartet. His oratorio *The Creation* is still performed throughout the world, and *The Seasons* is heard occasionally.

Mozart, who died at the age of thirty-five, was an infant prodigy. He played the harpsichord when he was four years of age, and composed his first piece, a minuet, when he was five. Mozart composed in every form known in his time. Haydn regarded him as the greatest composer of the age. Mozart's comic operas, *The Marriage of Figaro*, *Don Giovanni*, and *The Magic Flute* are still as fresh and sparkling as ever.

Towards the end of the eighteenth century the transition from the " classical " to the "romantic " period may be traced. The early works of Beethoven follow the same lines as Mozart's, but Beethoven's maturer works cover an infinitely greater range. His music portrays the different periods of his life. At first he clearly derived inspiration from Haydn and Mozart ; this is apparent from the early piano sonatas and the first two symphonies. The second period, when the *Appassionata* and *Moonlight* sonatas and symphonies number three to eight were written, was the happiest of his life, and he was able to develop his individuality to the full. During the last period, when the *Choral* symphony was written, Beethoven was afflicted with total deafness, and worry and domestic unhappiness overshadowed his existence.

Though Beethoven was one of the greatest composers, composition did not come easily to him. His musical sketch books show the immense pains he took to compose and revise his melodies.

Franz Schubert, unlike Beethoven, composed with very little effort ; melody seemed to come naturally to him. Schubert, who was born in very humble circumstances, was the world's greatest song-composer. Of a shy and retiring disposition, he was quite unable to " push " his music, which never received the recognition it deserved during his lifetime. Though he composed more than 600 songs he received a mere pittance and died in poverty at the age of 31, having been stricken with typhoid fever. Apart from his importance as a song-writer, Schubert wrote some charming instrumental music, including his *Unfinished Symphony*, a perfect example of the romantic in music.

Weber and Meyerbeer are important as operatic composers. Weber's *Euryanthe, Oberon, Der Freischütz,* and *Abu Hassan* provided the foundations of German opera as a national institution. Meyerbeer's flowing style brought the richness of Italian melody to the more solid German harmony.

At the beginning of the nineteenth century, Mendelssohn, Schumann and Chopin held the stage. Mendelssohn, though his music is often criticized as being over-sentimental, left us the exquisite *Midsummer Night's Dream* music, the *Songs without words*, and *Elijah*, an oratorio of great dramatic quality. Schumann's contributions to song-literature are as important as those of Schubert. Schumann wrote many charming piano works and some fine chamber music. His orchestral compositions were not so successful, for he did not appreciate the subtleties of orchestration. Chopin was one of the greatest pianists of his generation, and his *Preludes*, *Valses*, *Nocturnes* and *Mazurkas* are some of the most prized compositions in the modern pianist's repertoire.

Hector Berlioz, born in 1803, was a revolutionary in the musical world. Many of his ideas were impracticable, but he is chiefly important as the exponent of modern " programme " music ; music which sets out to tell a story or to portray an event.

Richard Wagner, a contemporary of Berlioz, was equally unconventional in his music. It is to Wagner that German opera owes most of its greatness. Wagner's early operas met with little success. He was nearly thirty when he wrote his first great work *Rienzi*, which was produced at the Dresden Opera House with enormous success. *Rienzi* was followed by *The Flying Dutchman*, *Tannhäuser* and *Lohengrin*. Wagner had sketched out *Die Meistersinger* when he became involved in a revolutionary movement, and was forced to flee from Dresden.

After a period of inactivity, Wagner was persuaded by his staunch friend, Liszt, to write a new series of operas, and he started work on an operatic version of an old legend *The Ring of the Nibelungs.* Wagner intended to divide the work into four sections, each a full length opera in itself : *Das Rheingold, Die Walküre, Siegfried,* and *Götterdämmerung.* Before *The Ring* was completed, *Die Meistersinger,* one of the finest comic operas ever written, was produced in Munich (1828).

In 1860 Wagner received a pardon and returned to Germany, where he married Cosima, daughter of Liszt, his first wife, Minna Planer, having died. At the invitation of Ludwig, King of Bavaria, he came to Munich to complete *The Ring,* which was later performed at a new theatre at Bayreuth, which had been specially erected for the purpose. Wagner's last work was *Parsifal,* a semi-religious drama, founded on the story of the Holy Grail. Wagner's literary education enabled him to write librettos to his operas which had real dramatic value ; hitherto opera librettos had nearly always been subordinated to the music.

After Wagner, opera flourished in France under Massenet, Saint-Saens, Thomas and Delibes, and in Italy under Verdi and Puccini.

During the latter part of the nineteenth century, Johannes Brahms was the last of the great composers to follow in the footsteps of the classical masters. Brahms imbued the symphonic form with new life, and his songs and chamber music are of first importance.

Liszt, who became the world's greatest pianist, is chiefly important for his influence on the composers of his day—his own compositions cannot be rated highly, but his enthusiasm for the rising school of composition, and his generous friendship and encouragement, was a source of inspiration to many of his more talented contemporaries.

Towards the middle of the nineteenth century, a school of nationalist composers arose. Schumann, in

1843, wrote:[1] "It really begins to look as if the nations bordering on Germany desired to emancipate themselves from the influence of German music; this might annoy a German nativist, but it would only appear natural and cheering to the more profound thinker, if he understood human nature. . . . Though they (the nationalist composers) all seem to regard Germany as their first and favourite teacher of music, we cannot wonder that they try to speak their own musical language to their own nation, without becoming untrue to their former instructor. For no land can yet boast of masters that equal our greatest ones; who will declare the contrary?"

Apart from literary and political motives, nationalism in music was greatly influenced by the rediscovery of folk-music. The influence of Czech folk-tune is clearly seen in the music of Smetana and Dvořak, and of Norwegian folk-tune in the music of Grieg; these composers did not so much imitate actual folk-tunes as create original themes in the spirit of folk-music. In Russia the Nationalist Movement was championed by Glinka, Borodin, Balakiref, Mussorgsky and Rimsky-Korsakof; the music of Tschaikovsky, Liadof, Arensky and Glazunof, and of younger men, Scriabin, Rachmaninof, Stravinsky and Prokofief, while retaining many of the characteristic features of the Russian style, is for the most part more cosmopolitan. The Spanish idiom, which was established in Europe in 1876, when Bizet's *Carmen* was produced (which, despite its French composer, has a picturesque Spanish flavour), is strongly felt in the music of Albéniz, Granados and Falla.

Following the age of Romanticism we come to the period of modern music, and the music of to-day. Here we find conflicting schools of thought—the Impressionists, led by Debussy and Ravel, whose music seeks to suggest

[1]Music and Musicians. Trans. Ritter.

emotion by vague and abstract means, much in the same way that the impressionist painter reproduces in colour patches the effect of light upon objects rather than the objects themselves in definite lines and surfaces; the late Romanticists, Mahler, Franck, Richard Strauss, Sibelius, Janáček, Wolf and Reger, whose music, while setting aside the old conceptions of form, key, concord and discord, and the like, still clings to the romantic ideal of direct expression of emotion; the Neo-Classicists, or Anti-Romanticists, Roussel, Stravinsky, Bartók and Hindemith, who seek to exclude from their music all external feeling or illustration, Stravinsky even directing that certain of his music be played without expression, so as to deprive it of anything likely to excite emotion; the Anti-Impressionists, Satie, Milhaud, Honneger and Poulenc; the New Nationalists, Bloch, Kodály, Ives, Harris, Copland, Prokofief, Enesco, Villa-Lobos, Chávez and Shostakovitch; the New Romanticists, Orff, Messiaen, Barber and Jolivet; the Twelve-Note composers, Schönberg, Berg, Webern, Křenik and Dallapiccola; the Electronic and Avant-Garde composers, Stockhausen, Boulez, Badings, Nillsson, Varèse, Berio and John Cage; and the Experimentalists, such as Iannis Xenakis and Peter Zinovieff, who have used computers as a means of composition.

CHAPTER XIV

THE MUSIC OF ENGLAND

The beginnings of English music must be looked for in the songs and dances of the common people, which we now call folk-songs and folk-dances. We have a very rich heritage of folk music, some of which has been passed on from generation to generation, and has been painstakingly collected by modern musicians. In particular, we owe a great debt to Cecil Sharp, who devoted himself to the discovery of folk music, searching every part of England in his quest, and founding the English Folk Dance Society for the revival of folk-dancing.

The early attempts at harmony would be considered very crude to-day. Choral melodies were often sung a fourth or a fifth apart, a practice known as "organum", which must have produced an effect little short of excruciating if long continued; try playing a melody on the piano with the two hands a fifth apart throughout, and judge for yourself. There are few early records of instrumental music, but from the practice, even up to Elizabeth's time, of playing vocal music on instruments, it would seem that both forms must have been vary much alike.

The earliest music worthy of serious attention is a "rota" or round in the Wessex dialect *Sumer is acumen in*, composed during the early part of the thirteenth century. This remarkable composition, with its flowing melody and complex structure, is an example without parallel in early music.

Under the Tudors, music began to be cultivated as an art. Henry VII, a great lover of music, encouraged musical teaching, and it was about this time that the degree of Doctor of Music was instituted at Cambridge University.

Elizabeth was keenly interested in music, and is said to have practised on the virginals assiduously, though we do not know whether or not she was a skilled performer. She was generous in patronizing the composers of her time, and supported the greatest of them, William Byrd, in spite of his adherence to the Roman faith during the rise of Protestantism. Byrd became a Gentleman of the Chapel Royal, sharing the duties of organist with another composer, Thomas Tallis, and in 1575 Elizabeth granted Byrd and Tallis the sole rights to print music and music paper. Byrd's sacred compositions are unsurpassed by those of any other composer of his time. He also wrote string and keyboard music (including the fine set of variations on the ballad *The Carman's Whistle*, still to be heard in modern programmes), and was one of the founders of the English Madrigal School.

Music now began to be cultivated in the home, and the "chest of viols", a set of stringed instruments of different sizes, was to be found in the homes of the nobility. Music for voices and viols became popular, and the ability to sing at sight was considered a necessary accomplishment for a gentleman of the period.

Even after Elizabeth's death, the Elizabethan school continued to flourish for some time under composers such as John Dowland, the greatest lute player of his age, whose songs with lute accompaniment are still occasionally heard; Dr. John Bull, the first music professor to be appointed at Gresham College, who is claimed by some to be the composer of *God Save the King*; and Orlando Gibbons, who was organist of the Chapel Royal of James I and also of Westminster Abbey, and who left some fine church music and music for viols and for virginals.

In Cromwell's time church music, which had become an important part of the services, suffered a severe setback. The Puritans forbade the singing of anthems and the playing of church organs, and hymns were only permitted to be sung in unison. But when Charles II came to the throne, church music was heard once more, and the theatres, which had been closed during the civil war, were opened again.

About the middle of the seventeenth century, opera was introduced in England. The first real opera, *The Siege of Rhodes*, was produced by Sir William Davenant at Rutland House, a hall in Charterhouse Yard, Aldersgate Street, which is said to have held some 400 people.

In 1659 Henry Purcell was born in London. This short-lived genius (he died at the age of thirty-six) is generally considered the first of the few great English composers. Purcell became a choirboy in the Chapel Royal, and seems to have received musical instruction from Captain Cooke, Pelham Humphrey and Dr. John Blow. He started his musical career as a tuner and repairer of organs and virginals. For many years he tuned the organ at Westminster Abbey, and was also employed there as a music copyist. In 1679 Purcell succeeded Blow as organist at the Abbey, where he composed the magnificent anthems *My Heart is Inditing* and *I was Glad* for the coronation of James II.

Purcell's first operatic attempt, *Dido and Aeneas*, was originally composed for a girls' boarding-school at Chelsea. It was followed by a number of successful compositions for the theatre, including the musical play *King Arthur*, which he wrote in collaboration with the poet Dryden. Purcell also composed church music, songs, and suites for harpsichord and other instruments. In 1694, the year of his death, he wrote the music for Queen Mary's funeral, which included the beautiful anthem *Thow Knowest, Lord, the Secrets of our Hearts.* It was performed at his own funeral eight months later. He was buried in Westminster Abbey.

In 1685 Johann Sebastian Bach and George Frederic Handel were born in Germany. Bach spent his life in the country of his birth, but Handel became a naturalized Englishman and lived for many years at his house in Brook Street, London.

Handel's father was a barber-surgeon who did not wish his son to adopt a musical career. Young Handel was therefore obliged to study in secret until the Duke of Weissenfels, recognizing the boy's great gifts, persuaded the father to allow him to take lessons with Zacha, organist of Halle Cathedral. Handel then went to Hamburg, where he was engaged as violinist at the Opera House. It was here that he produced his first opera *Almira.*

After a visit to Italy, Handel was appointed chief court musician to the Elector of Saxony. In 1710 Handel obtained permission to visit England to produce his opera *Rinaldo*, which he composed in two weeks. The opera was a great success and Handel, after returning to Hanover to attend to his duties, was soon back in England. This time he overstayed his leave, and so incurred the displeasure of the Elector when he came to the English throne as George I. Handel was restored to favour, so the story goes, by composing his *Water Music,* which was played at a water fête given by the King.

Handel now turned his attention to opera, and took an active part in an attempt (under the title of The Royal Academy of Music) to establish Italian opera in England. He wrote a number of operas for this venture, some of which met with considerable success. When the

fortunes of the Academy declined, Handel went into
partnership with Heidegger, lessee of the King's Theatre,
and later with Rich of Covent Garden Theatre, producing
several new operas ; but in spite of all his efforts both
companies became bankrupt. Of Handel's forty operas,
only a few airs and the celebrated *Largo* from *Serse*
survive.

Handel, now fifty, disillusioned by the failure of his
operas and a prey to overwork and paralysis of the hand,
devoted himself to oratorio. His first oratorios *Saul*
and *Israel in Egypt* were not at all well received, but
when *Messiah* was performed in London the audience
was deeply affected and, following the example of the
King, rose to its feet at the *Hallelujah Chorus*, a custom
which has been observed ever since. *Messiah* is still
Handel's best-loved work ; his other oratorios have
been rather neglected of late, and *Judas Maccabeus,
Samson, Alexander's Feast* and *Israel in Egypt* are far
too infrequently performed.

Towards the end of his life Handel's sight began to
fail. He soon became quite blind, although he still
continued to play the organ and to direct performances
of his works until a few days before his death on April
14th, 1759. Handel was impulsive, quick-tempered,
honorable in all his dealings and a sincere Christian. His
music, unlike that of Bach who was a master of intricate
detail, is characterized by its boldness and simplicity.

Among the factors which contributed to the failure
of Handel's operatic ventures was the production, in
1728, of *The Beggar's Opera*. With a wittily satirical
libretto by John Gay aimed at the conventions of
Italian opera, and sixty-nine favourite ballad-tunes
arranged by Dr. Pepusch, it took London and the
provinces by storm, and gave rise to a series of ballad

operas which temporarily eclipsed all other forms of stage production.

The last half of the eighteenth and first half of the nineteenth centuries were undistinguished periods of English musical history. Dr. Arne (1710-1778) deserves notice, and is chiefly remembered for his Shakespearean songs *Where the Bee Sucks* and *Blow, Blow Thou Winter Wind*, and for his song, *Rule, Britannia* (from the masque *Alfred*) of which Wagner remarked that the first eight notes expressed the whole character of the English people.

In 1767 the pianoforte was heard for the first time in England, and quickly came into general use. With the advent of this new instrument, capable of producing effects undreamt of by keyboard players, there arose a generation of pianist-composers. The first of importance is the Italian Clementi, who was brought over to England when a boy; a gifted composer, and one of the foremost teachers of his day, he is best known for his studies *Gradus ad Parnassum*. Another exceptional pianist-composer is John Field, born in Dublin in 1782, who attracted much attention by giving public recitals at the age of eight; Field's compositions were few, and he is chiefly remembered as the inventor of the Nocturne, a form which Chopin later developed with consummate skill.

In the latter half of the nineteenth century, the comic operas of Sullivan and incidental music of German set a new standard for light music which has never been surpassed. Parry, best known for his beautiful setting of Milton's *Blest Pair of Sirens*, and Stanford both contributed music of value, but the dominating figure of the period was Edward Elgar.

Elgar (1857-1934) was the son of an organist of a Worcester church who also had a music-selling business.

Much of Elgar's music became known through being performed at musical festivals. His *Enigma Variations* established him as a composer of the highest merit. *The Dream of Gerontius*, an oratorio setting of Cardinal Newman's poem, two symphonies, a violin concerto, a 'cello concerto, the *Cockaigne* overture and the *Pomp and Circumstance* marches are among his best works.

At the beginning of the twentieth century some of Elgar's younger contemporaries held the stage. Delius (1862-1934) produced a new kind of Romantic Impressionism. His music stands alone; it is characterized by a rare, whimsical beauty. *Over the Hills and Far Away, On Hearing the first Cuckoo in Spring, Paris, Brigg Fair* and *Summer Night on the River* all convey the composer's intensely personal impressions of the scenes.

Vaughan Williams (1872-1958), like Gustav Holst, began as a folk-song enthusiast. Soon his highly individual style began to assert itself, a style—robust and typically English—which he steadily developed. He left nine symphonies, concertos for violin, piano, oboe and bass tuba, numerous choral works and several operas, including *Hugh the Drover* (1914), *Sir John in Love* (1929), *The Poisoned Kiss* (1936) and *The Pilgrim's Progress* (1951). Other distinguished twentieth century composers include Holst (1874-1934), born at Cheltenham but Swedish by ancestry, composer of *The Planets* and *The Perfect Fool;* Coleridge-Taylor (1975-1912), son of a West African negro doctor and composer of the ever-popular *Song of Hiawatha;* Sir Arnold Bax (1883-1943), in whose symphonies Russian influences, as well as Irish characteristics, may be found; John Ireland (1879-1962), whose setting of Masefield's *Sea Fever* gained him wide popularity; Rutland Boughton (1878-1960), whose opera *The Immortal Hour* met with considerable success in London; Frank Bridge (1879-1941), whose eclectic style found its finest expresssion in chamber music; and Alan Rawsthorne (1905-1971), widely known for his *Symphonic Studies* and *Street Corner Overture*, who also composed three symphonies, two piano concertos and two violin concertos.

Outstanding among living composers are Sir Arthur Bliss (born in 1891), whose works include *A Colour Symphony*, a violin concerto, and the ballets *Adam Zero, Checkmate* and *Miracle in the Gorbals;* Sir William Walton (born in 1902), composer of two symphonies, the comedy overture *Portsmouth Point*, concertos for violin, viola and 'cello, *Façade*, two operas, and the remarkable oratorio *Belshazzar's Feast;* Edmund Rubbra (born 1901), composer of seven symphonies, several concertos, and much choral and chamber music; Michael Tippett (born in 1905), composer of the oratorio *A Child of Our Time*, two symphonies, a piano concerto, and the operas *The Midsummer Marriage* and *King Priam;* and Benjamin Britten (born 1913), surely the most distinguished English composer of his generation, whose opera *Peter Grimes*, first produced at Sadler's Wells in 1945, established him as an international figure. Britten's other works include the operas *The Rape of Lucretia, Albert Herring, Billy Budd, Gloriana, The Turn of the Screw* and *A Midsummer Night's Dream;* the *Spring Symphony, The Young Person's Guide to the Orchestra, Sinfonia da Requiem, Noye's Fludde*, concertos for piano, violin and 'cello, and *A War Requiem*, commissioned for the consecration festival at Coventry Cathedral in 1962.

CHAPTER XV

SUGGESTIONS FOR FURTHER STUDY

Nobody has ever learnt all there is to know about music. The study of music, like the study of literature, is inexhaustible ; there are always fresh fields to be explored, and new discoveries to be made. This is the charm of music, which, though it may change its form, never loses its appeal.

The musician, whether he is a singer, an instrumentalist, or a composer, should be ever eager to broaden his outlook by finding out things for himself. Though his first steps in music will naturally be confined to the study of a particular subject, as soon as he has made progress he should not confine his activities to a limited objective, but should roam over the whole field of music wherever his fancy takes him. Once he has started on the voyage of discovery he will never turn back.

For the seeker of musical knowledge there are thousands of books, old and new, and vast collections of music. He may even go back more than two thousand years to Aristotle, who wrote " Music, as everybody knows, is a delicious pleasure . . . it forms part of every social gathering and of every entertainment as a sheer delight." Or, delving at random, he may open Pepys' Diary for 1666 and read : " Discoursed with Mr. Hooke about the nature of musical sounds, and he did make me understand the nature of musical sounds made by strings, mighty prettily ; and told me that having come to a certain number of vibrations proper to make any tone, he is able to tell how many strokes a fly makes with her wings (those flies that hum in their flying) by the note that it answers to in music during their flying."

From the same source he may learn about "barber's music", music which used to be performed in barber's shops for the entertainment of the waiting customers.

Every music lover should know of *Grove's Dictionary of Music and Musicians*. This great work, now in ten volumes, may be consulted in most public libraries. The articles, each written by an expert, vary in length with the importance of the subject; that on Beethoven, for instance, occupies more than sixty pages. A smaller dictionary, which covers the whole field of music in one volume of some thousand pages, is *The Oxford Companion to Music;* the entire work is written and edited by Percy Scholes who, in consultation with experts, devoted many years to his immense task. From the same pen is *The Concise Oxford Dictionary of Music*, and *The Oxford Junior Companion to Music* (for young people aged 8 to 16).

Books that will Help You

Here is a list of books on practical subjects, and on history and appreciation, which you should read. They are written in a straightforward style which anyone can understand. Only those books which will really help you to study have been selected; those which give the maximum of information with the minimum of padding. Their number has been deliberately reduced to a minimum, because nowadays many people have little time for reading.

Piano Playing

> *Teach Yourself The Piano*—KING PALMER (Teach Yourself Books).
>
> *Musical Secrets*—LILIAS MACKINNON (Oxford University Press).

Both these books are clear and concise; the second, though tiny, contains an astonishing number of useful hints.

Accompanying at the Piano

The Unashamed Accompanist—GERALD MOORE (Methuen).
One of the very few books on Accompanying; excellent.

Singing

Teach Yourself Singing—C. R. THORPE (Teach Yourself Books).

The Organ

The Church Organist—HENRY COLEMAN (Oxford University Press).
Teach Yourself The Organ—FRANCIS ROUTH (Teach Yourself Books).

The Violin

Fiddling for Fun—ROBIN GILBERT (Faber).
A practical book for all amateur violinists.
Violin Playing as I Teach It—LEOPOLD AUER (Duckworth).

Chamber Music

Chamber Music—ed. ALEC ROBERTSON (Penguin Books).

Wind Instruments

Flute Technique—F. B. CHAPMAN (Oxford University Press).
Oboe Technique—EVELYN ROTHWELL (Oxford University Press).
Clarinet Technique—FREDERICK THURSTON (Oxford University Press).
Bassoon Technique—ARCHIE CAMDEN (Oxford University Press).
Horn Technique—GUNTER SCHULLER (Oxford University Press).
Trumpet Technique—D. A. DALE (Oxford University Press).
Recorder Technique—A. ROWLAND JONES (Oxford University Press.)

Musical History

The Growth of Music—H. C. COLLES (Oxford University Press).
The Listener's History of Music—PERCY SCHOLES (Oxford University Press).
A Concise History of Music—WILLIAM LOVELOCK (G. Bell & Sons).

These three books are among the best of all short histories of music.

Musical Appreciation and Listening

The Listener's Guide to Music—PERCY SCHOLES (Oxford University Press).

Opera

Concise Oxford Dictionary of Opera—ROSENTHAL & WARRACK (Oxford University Press).

English Music

A History of Music in England—ERNEST WALKER, Rev. J. A. WESTHRUP (Oxford University Press).

Dictionaries of Musical Terms

An ABC of Music—IMOGEN HOLST (Oxford University Press).

A concise general survey of all musical terms and ideas which are likely to confront the amateur musician.

A Student's Dictionary of Music—WILLIAM LOVELOCK (G. Bell & Sons).

An excellent small dictionary with over 2,000 entries, ranging from simple definitions of foreign terms to concise articles on important subjects.

INDEX

Abbreviations, 44–45
Absolute pitch, 3, 53
Abu Hassan, 167
Accent, 29, 31
Acciaccatura, 45
Accidental, 25, 162
Accompanying at the piano, 74–76
Adam Zero, 179
Albéniz, Isaac, 170
Alexander's Feast, 176
Alfred, 177
All through the night, 162, 163
Almira, 175
Alto clef, 26, 94
Amati family, 81
Ambrose of Milan, 161
American organ, 13–14, 16, 116
Appassionata sonata, 167
Appoggiatura, 45
Appreciation, musical, 143–144
Arco, 92
Arensky, A. S., 170
Aristotle, 150, 180
Arpeggio, 47
Arpeggios, how to play, 69–71
Arne, Dr. T. A., 177
Augmented intervals, 32–34

Bach, Johann Sebastian, 57, 114, 164, 165–166, 175
Badings, Henk, 171
Bailliff's Daughter of Islington, The, 163
Balakiref, M. A., 170
Banks, Benjamin, 81
Bar, 29–31
Barber, Samuel, 171
Barber's music, 181
Baritone, 124
Baritone clef, 26
Bar-line, 29, 162
Bartok, Béla, 171
Bass, 124
Bass clarinet, 10, 104, 152, 153
Bass clef, 21, 97

Bass drum, 154
Bassoon, 10–11, 15–16, 104–105, 150, 152, 153
Bax, Sir Arnold, 179
Beat, 29
Beethoven, Ludwig van, 57, 151, 156, 167
Beggar's Opera, The, 176
Bellows, harmonium, 14
Bells, 154
Belshazzar's Feast, 179
Berg, Alban, 171
Berio, Luciano, 171
Berlioz, Hector, 151–152, 168
Bible, music and the, 159–161
Binary form, 163
Biographia Literaria, 138
Bis, 45
Bizet, A. C. L., 170
Blest Pair of Sirens, 177
Bliss, Sir Arthur, 179
Bloch, Ernest, 171
Blow, John, 174
Blow, Blow thou Winter Wind, 177
Boatswain's Mate, The, 178
Boehm system, 98–99
Books, useful, 181–183
Borodin, A. P., 170
Boughton, Rutland, 178
Boulez, Pierre, 171
Bow, 'cello, 96
,,   viola, 95
,,   violin, 83, 87–88, 91–92, 95, 96
Brahms, Johannes, 169
Brass instruments, cost of, 18
,,   ,,   technique of, 16, 99–100
Breath control, 10, 102, 120–122, 127–129
Bridge, Frank, 179
Brigg Fair, 178
Britten, Benjamin, 179
Bull, Dr. John, 173
Burney, Dr. Charles, 77

Byrd, William, 173

Cage, John, 171
Carman's Whistle, The, 173
Carmen, 170
Castagnets, 117
'Cello playing, 9–10, 15, 95–97
Chalumeau, 103
Chamber music, 145—147
Chávez, Carlos, 171
Chest of viols, 173
Child of our Time, A, 179
Child Performer, The, 14–16
Chimes, 117
Chinese music, 158–159
Choir organ, 111
Chopin, Frédéric, 57, 168, 177
Choral singing, 131–133
Choral symphony, 151, 167
Chords, violin, 92
Chromatic scale, 44
Church organ, 110–114
Cinema organ, 116–117
Clarinet, 10–11, 15, 103–104, 150, 152–153, 155
Classics and Romantics, 166–167, 170
Clavichord, 57–58, 60
Clefs, C, 25–26
,,   Treble & Bass, 21, 26, 162
Clementi, M., 177
Cockaigne overture, 178
Coleridge, S. T., 138
Coleridge-Taylor, Samuel, 179
Combination pedals, 111
Competition Festivals, 132–133
Compound intervals, 34
,,   time, 30
Computer, composition by, 171
Concerto, 164
Conducting, 156–157
Console, 117
Continental fingering, 68
Contralto, 124
Copland, Aaron, 171
Cor anglais, 10, 103, 152, 153
Cornet,11-12,16,18,99,107,160
Cottage piano, 79

Couplers, 111, 115
Creation, The, 166
Crisofori, Bartolommeo, 59, 60
Crotchet, 26
Crooks, 106
Cross-fingering, 98
Cymbals, 117, 151, 154, 155
Czerny, Karl, 73

Da Capo, 45
Dallapiccola, Luigi, 171
Dal Segno, 45
Damper pedal, 64–68
Dampers, piano, 59–64–68, 79, 80
Davenant, Sir William, 174
David, 160
Debain, Alexandre, 114
Debussy, Claude, 170
Degrees of the scale, 44
Delibes, Leo, 169
Delius, Frederick, 178
Demisemiquaver, 27
Development, 164
Diatonic scale, 35
Dido and Aneas, 174
Diminished intervals, 32–33
Dominant, 44
Dona Nobis Pacem, 179
Don Giovanni, 166
Dots after notes, 27
,,   ,,   rests, 28
Double Bar, 29
Double-bass, 10, 15, 149, 151, 152, 154
Double-bassoon, 10, 151, 154
Double-flat, 24–25
Double-natural, 24
Double-sharp, 24–25
Double-tonguing, 101, 108
Dowland, John, 173
Dream of Gerontius, The, 178
Drums, 117, 149, 155
Duets, piano, 76–77
Dulcimer, 160
Duplet, 28
Duration of sound, how represented, 20, 26–28

Dvořak, Antonin, 170

Ear, importance of musical,
    8–9, 51
  ,, playing by, 54–55
Ear-training, 51–56
Egyptian music, 158
Electronic organ, 16, 116–117
Elgar, Edward, 177–178
Elijah, 168
Elizabeth, Queen, 149–173
Emotions, effect of music on
    the, 5–6
Emperor quartet, 147
Enesco, George, 171
English fingering, 65
  ,, Folk Dance Society, 172
  ,, horn, 10
  ,, music, 172–179
Enharmonics, 25
Enigma Variations, 178
Ensemble, 146
Essentials, 36
Euryanthe, 167
Exercises, ear-training, 55–56
  ,, singing, 133–134
Exposition, 164
Expression marks, 47–50
  ,, stop, 14, 115, 116

Falla, Manuel de, 170
Field, John, 177
Fine, 45
Fingering, 'cello, 96–97
  ,,   , double-bass, 97
  ,,   of wind instruments,
         98–105
  ,,   , piano, 68–71
  ,,   , viola, 94
  ,,   , violin, 88–91
Five-finger exercises, 63
Five Tudor Portraits, 179
Flat, 23–24
Flute, 10–11, 15, 18, 100, 149–
    150, 152–153, 155
Flying Dutchman, The, 168
Folk music, English, 172
Folk tune, 170

Form, 162–165
Forty-eight   Preludes   and
    Fugues, 57, 166
Franck, César, 171
Free reeds, 114
Freischütz, Der, 167
Fugue, 165
Full score, 144

Gay, John, 176
George I of England, 175
German, Edward, 177
Gibbons, Orlando, 173
Glazunof, Alexander, 170
Glinka, M.I., 170
Glockenspiel, 117, 154
Gluck, Christoph Willabald, 166
God Save the King, 173
Götterdämmerung, 169
Gradus ad Parnassum, 177
Gramophone, learning from
    the, 142–144
Granados, Enrique, 170
Grand Jeu, 115
Grand piano, 78
Great organ, 111
  ,, stave, 20
Greek music, 40, 149, 159
Gregory, Pope, 161
Grieg, Edvard, 170
Grove's Dictionary of Music, 181
Grupetto, 46
Guarneri family, 81
Guido d'Arrezzo, 161
Guitar, 109

Half note, 27
Hallelujah Chorus, 176
Handel, George Frederick, 114,
    160, 164, 175–176
Harmonic minor scale, 40–43
  ,,   series, 99–100
Harmonics, on brass instru-
    ments, 99–100
  ,,   violin, 91–92
Harmonium,   13–14,   16,
    114–116
Harmony, 5, 162

Harp, 16, 108–109, 149, 152–154, 159, 160
Harpsichord, 57–58, 149–150
Harris, Roy, 171
Haydn, Franz Joseph, 57, 147, 150–151, 166
Hearing, range of, 2
Henry VII, 172
Hindemith, Paul, 171
Holst, Gustav, 178, 179
Honneger, Arthur, 171
Horn, French, 11–12, 16, 99, 105–106, 150–152, 154–155
Hugh the Drover, 179

Immortal Hour, The, 179
Interpretation, 32–34
Intervals, 32–34
    ,, , augmented, 32–34
    ,, , diminished, 32–34
    ,, , major, 32–34
    ,, , minor, 32–34
    ,, , perfect, 32–34
Inverted intervals, 33–34
    ,, turn, 46
Ireland, John, 179
Israel in Egypt, 176
Ives, Charles, 171
I was glad, 174

Janáček, Leoš, 171
Job, 179
Jolivet, André, 171
Judas Maccabeus, 176

Keyboard, diagram of piano, 61
    ,, instruments, early, 57–58
    ,, position at the piano, 61
Key-note, 36–38, 44
Key-signature, 25, 36
Key-signatures table of, 25
King Arthur, 174
King, Chinese musical instrument, 158
King Priam, 179
Kodály, Zoltán, 171

Knee swells, 116
Křenek, Ernst, 171
Largo from Serse, 176
Leading note, 44
Leger lines, 22
Liadof, Anatole, 170
Lines and spaces, 20–21
Liszt, Franz, 62, 168, 169
Lohengrin, 168
London symphony, 150, 179
Lower mordent, 46
Lulli, Giovanni Battista, 156
Lunga Pausa, 28
Lyre, 149

Macdowell, E. A., 171
Magic Flute, The, 166
Mahler, Gustav, 171
Major scale, 35–39
Marriage of Figaro, The, 166
Massenet, J. E. F., 169
Mass in B minor, 166
Manuals, organ, 110–114
Mazurkas (Chopin), 168
Measure, definition of a, 29
    ,, , duple, triple and quadruple, 30
Mediant, 44
Meistersinger, Die, 169
Melodic minor scale, 40–43
Melody, 4, 14, 29
Memory, musical, 55
    ,, training, the, 137–139
Mendelssohn-Bartholdy, Felix, 57, 168
Messiaen, Olivier, 171
Messiah, 176
Meyerbeer, Jacob, 167–168
Mezzo-soprano, 123–124
    ,, clef, 26
Middle C, 21, 63
Midsummer Marriage, The, 179
Midsummer Night's Dream, A, 168
Milhaud, Darius, 171
Minim, 27
Minor scale, 35, 40–44

Miriam the prophetress, 159–160
Modes, 40, 161
Modulation, 163–164
Monteverdi, Claudio, 149
Moonlight sonata, 167
Mordent, 45–46
Moses, 159
Moscheles, Ignaz, 62
Mozart, Wolfgang Amadeus, 57, 101, 103, 156, 166, 167
Music as a social accomplishment, 7
,, , definition of, 1
Musico da camera, 146
Mussorgski, M. P., 170
Mute, horn, 106
,, , trumpet, 4
,, , violin, 93
My Heart is Inditing, 174

Nationalism in music, 169–171
Natural, 23–24
Nervousness, how to overcome, 139
Nillsson, Bo, 171
Nocturnes (Chopin), 57, 168, 177
Norfolk Rhapsodies, 178–179
Notation, 161–162
Notes, 20
Noye's Fludde, 179

Oberon, 167
Oboe, 10–11, 18, 102, 149–150, 153, 155
Octave, 22
Octave flute, 101
On hearing the first Cuckoo in Spring, 178
Opera, 164, 168–169, 174
Oratorio, 166, 176, 178, 179
Orchestra, beginning of the, 148–149
,, , eighteenth century, 149–151
,, , modern symphony, 151–153

Orfeo, 149
Orff, Carl, 171
Organ, introduction of the, 159, 161, 162
,, pedals, 13, 110–116
,, stops, 13, 110–113
,, technique, 12–13, 16, 110–114
Organum, 172
Ornaments, musical, 44–47
Overblowing, 100
Over the Hills and Far Away, 178
Oxford Companion to Music, The, 77, 181

Paris, 178
Parry, Sir Hubert, 177
Parsifal, 169
Pause, 28
Pedal-board, 13, 116
Pedal organ, 13, 111, 114
Pedalier, 13
Pedalling, art of piano, 65–68
Pedals, harp, 109
,, organ, 13, 110–114
,, piano, 13, 54–68
Pepusch, Dr., 176
Pepys, Samuel, 73, 180
Percussion instruments, 151, 153–155
Personality in solo singing, 129–131
Peter Grimes, 179
Phrasing marks, 31
Piano, choosing a, 78–79
,, compass of the, 60
,, cost of a, 17
,, invention of the, 59–60
,, looking after a, 79–80
,, playing the, 8, 15, 61–63
,, popularity of the, 8
,, quartet, 147
,, quintet, 147
,, repertory of the, 57
,, tuning, 80
Piano-conductor, 156

Piccolo, 10, 101, 151–153
Pipes of Pan, 160
Pipes, organ, 110
Pistons, 99–100
Pitch, definition of ,2
Pitch, new philharmonic, 52
,,   representation of, 20
Pitchpipe, 51–52
Pizzicato, 92
Placing the voice, 105
Planer, Minna, 169
Planets, The, 179
Poisoned Kiss, The, 179
Pomp and Circumstance
    marches, 178
Portability of instruments, 18
Portsmouth Point, 179
Positions, violin, 90
Poulenc, Francis, 171
Practice, annoyance caused by,
    18
,,   , importance of regular,
    19
,,   , how to, 61, 135–141
Preludes (Chopin), 168
Primo, 77
Programme music, 168
Prokofief, S., 170, 171
Psaltery, 160
Purcell, Henry, 174
Puccini, Giacomo, 169
Pythagoras, 161

Quadruplet, 28
Quarter note, 27
Quartet, 164
Quartet in D major (Tschai-
    kovsky), 147
Quaver, 26
Quintet, 164
Quintuplet, 28

Rachmaninof, Sergei, 170
Radio, learning from the,
    142–145
Ravel, Maurice, 170
Recapitulation, 164
Reed, bassoon, 11, 105

Reed, clarinet, 11, 104
,,   oboe, 11, 101
Reed-pipe, 119–120
Reger, Max, 114, 171
Registration, organ, 111, 113
Relative keys, 41–42
Repeats, 45
Rests, 28
Rheinberger, J. G., 114
Rheingold, Das, 169
Rhythm, 4
Rienzi, 168
Rimsky-Korsakof, Nicholas A,,
    170
Rinaldo, 175
Ring of the Nibelungs, The, 169
Roman music, 149
Roussel, Albert, 171
Rubbra, Edmund, 179
Rule Britannia, 177

St. Matthew Passion, 166
Saints-Saëns, Charles Camille,
    169
Samson, 176
Sancta Civitas, 179
Satie, Erik, 171
Saul, 176
Saxophone, 11
Scale, birth of the, 161–163
Scales, how to play, 69–70
,,   major and minor, 35–
    43
Schönberg, Arnold, 171
Schubert, Franz, 101, 147, 155,
    167
Schumann, Robert, 57, 62,
    168, 169
Score-reading, 144
Scriabin, Alexander, 170
Sea Fever, 179
Seasons, The, 166
Secondo, 78
Semibreve, 26
Semiquaver, 26
Sextet, 146, 164
Sextolet, 28
Septolet, 28

Shake, 46
Shamus O'Brien, 177
Sharp, 23–24
,, Cecil, 172
Shostakovitch, Dmitri, 171
Sibelius, Jean, 171
Side Drum, 145
Siege of Rhodes, The, 174
Siegfried, 169
Sight-reading, 138–141
Silent bars, 45
Simple time, 30
Sinfonia da Requiem, 179
Singing, reasons, for, 7, 8
,, technique of, 118–134
Single-tonguing, 102
Sir John in Love, 179
Sleigh bells, 117
Slur, 32
Smetana, Friedrich, 170
Smyth, Dame Ethyl, 178
Soft pedal, 64
Solomon, 160
Solos, how to play piano, 71–72
Sonata, 164
,, form, 164–165
Songs of Hiawatha, The, 179
Songs, solo, 134
Songs without words, 168
Soprano, 123
,, clef, 26
Sound, definition of, 1–2
,, of wind instruments, 11
,, power of, 2–3
,, quality of, 3–4
Spinet, 57–58, 60
Staccato, 32
Stanford, Sir Charles Villiers, 177
Stave, 20, 21, 162
Stockhausen, Karlheinz, 171
Stop-keys, 117
Stopped horn notes, 106
Stops, American organ, 14, 116
,, , church organ, 13, 110–114
,, , cinema organ, 117
,, , harmonium, 14, 114–115

Strachey, Lytton, 142
Stradivari, Antonio, 81
Strauss, Richard, 171
Stravinsky, Igor, 170, 171
String adjuster, 84
String quartet, 146–147
Strings, viola, 95
,, violin, 83–84
Subdominant, 44
Submediant, 44
Sullivan, Sir Arthur, 177
Sumer is acumen in, 172
Summer Night on the River, 178
Supertonic, 44
Swell, organ, 110–111
,, pedal, 110
Symphony, 163, 164
Syncopation, 31

Tabret, 160
Tallis, Thomas, 173
Tambourine, 154, 159
Tannhäuser, 168
Tape recorder, 145
Tausig, Karl, 137
Tchaikovsky, Peter Ilitch, 147, 170
Tenor, 123–125
,, clef, 26, 97
Terms, glossary of musical, 47–50
Ternary form, 163
Theatres, closing of the, 174
Thomas, Ambroise, 169
Thou Knowest, Lord, the Secrets of our Hearts, 175
Tie, 31
Timbre, 3
Timbrel, 159
Time, 29–30
,, beating, 156
,, signatures, 29–30
Timpani, 150, 153–154
Tippett, Michael, 179
Tone, 23
Tone-colour, 3, 4, 14, 68, 144, 147, 155
Tone production, violin, 91

Tonic, 44
,, minor, 44
,, sol-fa, 43–44
Touch, piano, 53-54
Treble clef, 21, 26, 94
Tre corda, 68
Tremolo, stop, 113
Triangle, 151, 154
Trill, 46
Trio, chamber, 146, 164
Triplet, 27
Triple-tonguing, 101, 108
Trombone, 11–12, 16, 18, 100, 107–108, 149, 150–152, 154
Trout quintet, 147
Trumpet, 11–12, 16, 99, 106, 149–150, 152, 154, 159
Tuba, 11–12, 99, 108, 152–154
Tudor music, 172–173
Tuning, 'cello, 95
,, double-bass, 97
,, viola, 84
violin, 74–85
Tuning-fork, 51–52, 79
Turn, 46
Una corda, 68
Unfinished Symphony, 155, 167
Unison, 33
Upper mordent, 45–46
Upright piano, 78–79

Valses (Chopin), 57, 168
Valves, 99–100
Varése, Edgar, 171
Variation form, 164
Vaughan Williams, Ralph, 161, 178
Verdi, Giuseppi, 169
Vibrations, 1–2
Villa-Lobos, Heitor, 171
Viol, 149, 160–161

Viola, cost of a, 17
,, playing, 9–10, 15
Violin, choosing a, 82
,, , cost of a, 17
,, , different sizes, 15
,, , history of the, 81
,, , playing, 9, 15, 93–103
Violin-conductor, 156
Virginal, 57–58
Vocal cords, 119–120
Voice, developing the, 9, 119–121
Voices, classification of, 122–125
,, boys and girls, 125
Voix celeste, 113
Volta, 1ma and 2nda, 45
Vox humana, 113

Wagner, Richard, 151–152, 168–169
Wagner, Cosima, 169
Walküre, Die, 169
Walton, William, 179
Water Music, The, 175
Weber, Carl Maria von, 167
Webern, Anton, 171
Where the Bee Sucks, 177
Whole note, 27
Wind instruments, cost of, 18
Wolf, Hugo, 171
Wolf notes, 95
Woodwind, instruments, technique of, 10–11, 15–16, 98
Words, how to sing, 126–127
Wreckers, The, 178

Xenakis, Iannis, 171
Xylophone, 117

Zinovieff, Peter, 171